GRIT, GROWTH AND *Gumption* FOR WOMEN:

Three Keys to Lead Yourself and Others With Confidence

TINSLEY ENGLISH

Defining Moments Press

Contents

Early Praise for Grit, Growth and Gumption for Women — 1

Important Note to the Reader — 4

Dedication — 5

The Coaster — 7

Greetings and Salutations — 9

PART ONE — 11

1. What No One is Telling You — 13

2. Leadership Myths Debunked — 21

3. We've Come a Long Way Baby, or Have We? — 25

4. Defining Your NorthStar Goal — 29

5. Introducing G-Force: From Carousel to Coaster — 43

PART TWO — 57

6. The Grit Factor: It's All About the Climb — 59

7. The Growth Factor: Lean Into the Turns — 93

8. The Gumption Factor: The Summit and Beyond — 123

PART THREE — 141

9. Bringing It All Together to Unleash Your G-Force   143

10. The Grace Factor: A Parting Gift   147

Words to Live By   149

Acknowledgements   154

Meet the Author   156

Notes   158

About   160

Defining Moments   162

Other #1 Bestselling Books   163

Early Praise for Grit, Growth and Gumption for Women

"When it comes to books on leadership, Tinsley nailed it. An expert in the field, her fresh approach and actionable strategies put women in the driver's seat of their own careers. If you are ready to lead with confidence, this is the book for you!"

—Gabrielle Bosché, 2x TEDx Speaker and CEO of The Purpose Company

"Tinsley's ability to articulate real-life experiences with practical application tools found in this book will be a valuable asset to readers in all phases of their career journey."

—Elyse Davis, Director of Regional Economic Development, Georgia Power Company

"Your book changed my entire mindset and brought me back to what I really care about in my career, which is helping my team around me be the best we can be. As someone in her late 20's, the book brought me out of my work bubble and reminded me who I am. I needed this not only to change my mindset but now I have the tools, advice, and support to manifest this destiny for myself and my colleagues. This book not only taught me skills that I can use in my personal life and work, but it encouraged me to have more confidence in myself."

—Karyna Pillay, Operations Associate, Hoffman Financial Group

"I was so excited to begin reading Grit, Growth and Gumption for Women. I could not put it down. From the first page, Tinsley prepares the reader for what to expect during the reading, giving just enough information to pique interest, while also leaving the reader asking, 'How in the world will I become a better leader?' And then she tells you. She shares first-hand experiences, letting the reader know they are not alone in any leadership mistakes they've made, and that improvement, even as drastic as a 180° turn, is possible. It's exciting, gripping and full of instruction. If you are a woman in leadership, read Tinsley's book. Your future and the people you lead will thank you."

—Kim Gunnells, Director of Recruiting, Black Lotus Financial

"Grit, Growth and Gumption (GGG) is a great motivating resource for every female to identify what it takes to be a good leader, a good person and where you want to take yourself. Tinsley has put the female perspective into a genuine and witty read that allows you to divide and conquer your career development into three categories: Grit, Growth and Gumption. GGG shows how determination and perseverance can aid in your leadership, your character and your personal brand. She sets the stage for the mindset of what is needed to be a good leader, how to set goals and track your progress and how to follow your gut with calculated risk. Her workbook style coaches you on how to identify what strengths and weaknesses exist for you and what steps you can take to improve your brand, your team and/or your next opportunity. A great read for the novice and tenured female leaders alike."

—Karen Waslawski, CIC, CPRIA, Strategist & Business Development, National Sales Leader

"In Grit, Growth & Gumption for Women, Tinsley offers a refreshing perspective on leadership that emphasizes authenticity and purpose. With a wealth of experience coaching and leading women, she provides practical insights and actionable strategies for aspiring leaders. One of the book's strengths is its focus on self-awareness and emotional intelligence as essential components of effective leadership. This book is a must-read for anyone looking to enhance their leadership skills and make a positive impact in their organization. English's insightful guidance and emphasis on authenticity and purpose set this book apart as a valuable resource for aspiring and seasoned leaders alike. You will find yourself applying the ideas and concepts in professional conversations immediately!"

—Ronna DeMichael, Instructional Coach

"This read takes you back to basics and instills good firm confidence. The examples and the techniques are spot on. It makes you feel good and want to express your leadership skills and knowledge and gain more to express and share. Love it!!"

—Trinisha Chambers, Underwriting Specialist, Liberty Mutual Insurance

Important Note to the Reader

This book contains exercises and journal prompts.
Download Your Free GGG Workbook here:
gritgrowthgumption.com/workbook

Dedication

To the incredible women who have come before me. Thank you! Your unwavering strength and courage serve as a guiding light for future generations. Your footsteps have paved the way for us to find inspiration, resilience and the power of the human spirit. Your legacy is woven into the fabric of history, reminding us of the countless barriers you shattered and the countless dreams you dared to pursue.

To the women who are currently on their path: Keep going! Hold fast to your dreams and aspirations in the face of challenges and uncertainties. Know that you have an unfathomable reservoir of strength and determination within you. You are not alone as a community of sisters stands beside you, ready to lift and cheer you on.

To the women who are just beginning their journey: Get excited! Embrace this moment with open arms as it is your chance to make a difference and leave an indelible mark on the world. As you climb the threshold of possibility, remember that the road ahead may be full of obstacles, but it is also lined with opportunities just waiting to be seized. Believe in yourself, trust in your abilities and let your passion be the guiding star that leads you forward.

This book is a tribute to women's strength, resilience and boundless potential everywhere. Let us honor the past, empower the present and inspire the future.

The Coaster

Grit grows like a roller coaster's rise,

Through twists and turns, life's grand surprise.

Leadership, a ride of highs and lows,

Gumption fuels the journey as it grows.

A NorthStar gleams, a constant guide,

In chaos, resilience is our stride.

Triumphs and trials, the coaster's track,

Growth blossoms, pushing us forward, not looking back.

Life's leadership, a thrilling quest,

With each challenge, we rise to the test.

Embracing change, we discover strength anew,

In leadership's rhythm, we evolve, unique and true.

Greetings and Salutations

Thank you for picking up this book today!

Did you know that you were born to lead? It's true! As women, we naturally possess the skills that lend to impactful leadership, such as listening, communication and empathy. One of my favorite things to do over the last two decades is to teach women that everyone has a leader within us. We show up on the front lines as role models for our families, in our industries and in our communities. We do not need a degree or certification to be called a leader, but there is a specific set of skills that will help you lead with confidence.

In my early days, I helped women the only way I knew how: by touting the benefits of hard work and dedication. I'd throw in anecdotes like "work smarter, not harder" or "believe in the power of positivity." While this was great advice, something was missing and I couldn't quite figure it out!

What I learned after much trial and error would change how I lead and approach my life. Hard work is just the tip of the iceberg and will only take you so far. Faking positivity not only makes you appear disengaged but also prevents you from dealing with the situation effectively as you're not being honest with yourself or others.

We are here with each other because, after spending the last 20 years failing forward in business and in life, I am confident that I have cracked the Code of Confident Leadership. While extremely simple, this Code will transform how you lead to ensure you achieve a career that leaves a legacy in each life you touch.

Even though we've only known each other for a few sentences, I want to let you in on a little secret: It might not seem like it now, but you already possess the three keys required to succeed as a leader! We need to identify the areas where your "tank is low" and optimize them! When you start running on all cylinders, you'll find the challenges you face can be handled with confidence that can only come from truly knowing yourself.

This book is a collection of hard-fought battles, triumphs and failures. I've filled these pages with my own stories and those in my G-Force Tribe. The women in my tribe come from all walks of life. From a former banking executive to a flight nurse, their stories will inspire you. These women have gone before you to blaze trails and put out fires, hoping the road you are on is a little less rocky and much more fun.

Another reason we were brought together is that I have made A LOT of mistakes in my career. I've left companies prematurely because I was too scared to ask for a raise. I have been passed over for promotions without solid reasons. I have faced severe health challenges. I have created new roles for myself and elevated leaders. Heck, I even quit corporate America for a minute to work on a dude ranch! By sharing my stories and those of the fantastic collection of women in my network, we can make the load lighter and the journey swifter for you.

This book is my gift to you in the hope that by finding the clarity you desire, you'll turn around and help the next woman.

So, my new friend, if you are ready to unlock the Code and unleash your power, let's get to it!

PART ONE

Grit, Growth and Gumption for Women:

Three Keys To Lead Yourself and
Others With Confidence

Chapter One

What No One is Telling You

What would your life look like if you already had achieved your ultimate career goals?

I have posed this question to dozens of female colleagues over the past several years and you would be surprised how many of them cannot describe that life in detail.

They might have a short-term idea of what the next few years would look like if they kept working at the same pace in the same role. Many of these women already held solid positions with prospects of future promotions. They may have applied for more prominent roles but were passed over for another candidate, even a peer. They may have led a team only to discover that their colleagues considered them more of a manager than a leader.

Yet no one has spelled out to these women in **black and white** why they were not chosen or what they were missing to lead with impact. They might have heard, "You still have unfinished business in your current role," or "You're not ready to lead a large team."

These are hard pills to swallow and would leave anyone scratching their head.

After such a blow, some will immediately update their resume and hop into the job market, while others will return to their current role, still wondering what they are "missing."

The problem is this: **one** missing key could be the barrier preventing them from achieving a great position, bouncing back from a failed project, or forging a strong connection with their team. They have seen other women break through the "glass ceiling" or build teams that would follow them anywhere but wonder why they are still struggling and feeling unfulfilled. The bigger problem is this: by failing to address that **one** key, they risk missing future opportunities or, worse, arriving at a career destination that doesn't remotely resemble what they envisioned.

I wrote this book for the woman giving it her all—putting in the long hours, consistently going above and beyond, tap dancing in high heels. For the woman who is the first to log on and the last to log off. The one who is always called to clean up the mess but never asked for her ideas to prevent the mess from occurring. The woman who lies in bed at 1 a.m. wondering what more she can give. The woman who has put herself out there, has taken an opportunity to assume a more significant role but still has not broken through the surface or been allowed to sit at the table.

If this doesn't sound like you, please return this book and I will happily refund your money!

If it does, congratulations!

By selecting this book, you have taken the first step toward recognizing that you have more to offer this world. You are a unique being placed here for a purpose, and I will do my best to help you begin to fulfill it!

World-renowned author and motivational speaker Ken Blanchard once stated, "Leadership is not about you. It's about investing in the growth of others." Ken makes an excellent point as we've all known those leaders who thought the sun rose and set around their egos. I like to add to Ken's sentiment that "Leadership is not only about you. It is about investing in the growth of yourself and others." You see, to lead others confidently, you need to understand how to lead yourself.

What Makes This Book Unique?

Do me a favor and run a quick Internet search on "leadership books for women." What did you come up with? Over 100,000 results, correct? And within those results, you will find books highlighting issues plaguing our gender, such as unconscious bias or pay equity. You will find books with colorful pink covers on "girl power" or "boss girl" mentality. You will find books that show you how to adapt your behavior to fit within the traditional "man's world." You will find books filled with hundreds of pages of statistics and science.

You are holding this book in your hands because after searching high and low for the wisdom I needed, I came up short in my quest for truth. What I needed did not exist. What I needed was an honest conversation about what I **could** control. At the end of the day, our attitudes and actions are the only elements within our ultimate control. This does not mean I do not place immense importance on society's responsibility to continue to "level the field," because I do. And do I love some girl power splashed with pink? You bet! Are statistics and science critical in supporting an idea? Most definitely! However, my mission was different. I wanted to create a guide for the woman who wants to take control of her future today and do it in a way that feels authentic to her.

I also learn things more quickly if I see them in practice rather than theory. This is why I will introduce you to Sarah, an emerging leader at a Fortune 500 insurance company. While Sarah is a fictitious person, she is the culmination of the personality traits of many emerging female leaders and will serve as an example as we work through the exercises in each chapter. We'll help guide Sarah along the way as she encounters challenges, and I'll include some of my Tribe's "war stories" as examples. We'll wrap up our time with her exploring the lessons she learned along the way.

And, hey, if you are anything like me, you want someone to get to the point quickly and provide practical, straightforward advice. The great news is that you can read this book in one sitting or in less than a week and begin to use the tools immediately.

So here is my vow to you: I will deliver on a few promises in each part of the book:

In Part One, I will:

- Debunk common leadership myths.

- Highlight a few of the challenges we are up against as females. Trigger warning: It is not pretty.

- Help you pinpoint your **NorthStar Goal.**

- Introduce you to a system that is designed to assist you in identifying your barriers and unleashing your power and potential.

In Part Two, I will:

- Explore the keys of grit, growth and gumption in greater detail.

- Provide strategies for each of the elements that make up these three keys.

- Highlight "Tribal Wisdom" strategies from women in my G-Force Tribe network who are changing the script on female leadership.

In Part Three, I will:

- Explain how grit, growth and gumption intersect to provide synergy.

- Send you off with an amazing parting gift. No peeking!

Before we dive in, I want to give you a few tips to start your journey off on the right foot:

Tip #1:

Read the entire book! Did you know that most people only get through the first three chapters of a book? It's true! A recent study showed that more than half of adults (51.57 percent) haven't read a full book in over a year [1]. Why am I telling you this? The purpose is twofold: (1) Truth: I've been known to place a book back on the shelf half-read more than once, so I get it. (2) Since the concepts in this book build on one another, I promise to make each chapter stimulating and fun, but it is up to you to read the entire book. Otherwise, you may miss the one key that unlocks your power.

Tip #2:

You can mistreat this book a little! Write in it, scribble notes, highlight it! The best books I own are covered in food and coffee stains. I will not be offended in the least if this book ends up looking like a preschooler's first coloring book. Bottom line: I want you to use it as your guidebook for years and not shelve it! Bonus: I've also included the link to a downloadable workbook so you can record your thoughts and measure your progress.

A word of caution: I will get "real, real!" I will share a few secrets along the way; please don't judge! I want to be completely transparent and ask that you do the same for yourself. When we move into the assessment phase in Chapter 5, I will ask you to rank yourself in several areas. I will also ask that you provide the assessment to three individuals who are close to you. They can be a friend, a partner, or coworker. Typically, a mix of all three will yield a consistent result. Your hard-wired traits tend to present themselves no matter the setting.

Tip #3:

Check your mindset! Adopting a receptive and open mindset is necessary as you delve into the words and guidance laid out before you. Allow yourself to challenge preconceived notions, embrace vulnerability and remain open to the prospect of change. Reflect on your attitudes, beliefs and perceptions, questioning whether they serve your personal growth or impede you.

Buckle up, sis. Here we go!

Chapter Two

Leadership Myths Debunked

"Leadership is doing the right thing even when it can be difficult."
—*Noel Abdur-Rahim*

While I told you early on that we as women are born to lead, I want to caution that leadership is not for the faint of heart. In fact, it can be downright lonely and challenging at times. There are days when I think I have it all figured out and others where I feel like I've let my team and the world down—deep sigh. In my early days, I operated under several common misconceptions about the word "leader" and what it meant:

Myth #1: Hard Work Is Enough

When I began managing a small team in my early 30s, I thought they would mirror my behavior if they saw me working hard. Do what I do. Keep your head down. Grind. Shouldn't that be enough?

Not quite. As my team arrived at work each morning, they would find me there banging away on my keyboard. I was pumped full of caffeine by that point and would immediately begin cataloging all the items I had tackled that morning or loading each one of my team members down with a new set of tasks for the day. No "hello" or "How was your weekend?" No "Is there anything you need from me today?" Of course not! There were things to do, clients to serve and no time for chit-chat!

I also had an annoying habit of playing the work martyr. If I did take a few minutes to grab another cup of coffee, I would take every opportunity to tell anyone who would listen how late I had stayed the night before or how much work was still left on my desk that day. I cringe when I hear this happening today as I know no one cares! Each person has sacrificed to get their work done, and my sob story did nothing but add to any stress they might be experiencing that day.

Truth

While you want your team to see you put in the effort, there is so much value in showing them that you realize it is not just about the work. Why not take a few minutes each day to check in on them? Ask about their plans for the weekend or discuss the latest Netflix series everyone is binging. These moments provide an opportunity to learn more about the person outside of the office and can deepen the connection within the team.

Myth #2: You Don't Need to Learn to Lead

Once I reached the VP level, I made the dangerous assumption that I had arrived equipped with all the tools I needed to lead my team successfully. Show me to the stage! Not quite. My team needed me to show up ready to relate to their struggles and actively listen to their ideas. Unfortunately, what they got was someone micromanaging every project or asking questions like, "Why would you do it that way?" Even worse, I might take a project back or withhold future assignments, figuring it was easier to do it myself.

I would also send what I perceived as clear communication on accomplishing a task, only to find that I left out a critical step. When they came to me for help, I would push them off, saying, "We'll get to that later," meaning they would have to wait until I was ready to discuss it.

I would even have days where my team and I would work within 10 feet of each other and not utter a single word, only communicating via email. Highly effective management style, right?

Truth

As you progress in your leadership journey, there is even more responsibility on your part to invest in your skills to ensure you are equipped to lead each person on your team individually. While a portion of this wisdom will come with time, it will also be up to you to seek out learning opportunities that challenge your ideas.

Myth #3: You Need Permission to Lead

This wisdom comes from my friend Ukeme Awakessien Jeter, who immigrated to the United States at 18 to attend college. Today, she is a partner at a national law firm, an elected official, and a sought-after speaker on Immigrant Leadership Development. Her work is informed by her unique perspective as a triple minority (black, female, immigrant), a mechanical engineer with an MBA and a lawyer. Ukeme has found that women and marginalized groups feel the need to wait for external validation or permission to lead.

Truth

Permission is optional. Authentic leadership comes when you learn to take risks and own the outcomes, even when the results are unfavorable. To lead fearlessly, women must learn to make decisions, pursue roles and take initiative. This is the definition of fearless leadership.

By understanding the common myths, you will be better prepared to receive the tools outlined in the coming chapters.

But first, let's investigate some statistics.

Chapter Three

We've Come a Long Way Baby, or Have We?

"Any society that fails to harness the energy and creativity of
its women is at a huge disadvantage in the modern world."
—Tian Wei

The Ceiling Was Just the Beginning

Enter any conversation on female leadership and you will likely hear a reference to the "glass ceiling," a term coined by Marilyn Loden, a management consultant at the New York Telephone Co. She used this expression during a panel discussion at the Women's Exposition in New York in 1978. Loden's motivation came from her research at work, where she was tasked with investigating the scarcity of women in executive roles. Her findings pointed to what she termed an "invisible barrier" that impeded women's progress in climbing the corporate ladder.

This idea underscored the longstanding challenges faced by women and minorities in the workplace. A few classic examples of this phenomenon include missing out on a promotion to a managerial role due to pregnancy or being reassigned to different projects to provide better opportunities for male colleagues.

Fast forward almost half a century and we find that while companies are making modest progress in elevating women to leadership positions, there is still a long way to go. According to the 2023 McKinsey "Women in the Workplace Study"[2], while women are still unrepresented at the corporate level, the number of women at the C-Suite level has increased from 17 percent to 29 percent since 2015, with more representation at the VP and SVP levels. While this presents a bright spot, the study also revealed that only 1 in 4 top C-Suite leaders in companies are women: for women of color, that number is just 1 in 16. As women of color climb the career ladder, their representation drops significantly—by two-thirds!

The study also debunked several myths:

Myth #1: Female Ambition is Waning

- **Truth:** Women show the same dedication to their careers and desire for promotions as men at every level of the job hierarchy, with 9 in 10 under age 30 wanting promotions and 3 in 4 aspiring to be senior leaders. Women of color are even more ambitious, with 96 percent valuing their careers and 88 percent aiming for the next level.

Myth #2: The Glass Ceiling Is My Biggest Barrier

- **Truth:** The Broken Rung is a more significant issue. In a typical company, men hold 60 percent of manager-level positions, leaving only 40 percent for women. This shortage makes it harder for women to advance, especially early-career Black women who face challenges in promotions.

Myth #3: Microaggressions Aren't a Big Deal

- **Truth:** While often dismissed, the impacts are real. Asian women are seven times more likely to be misidentified by race or ethnicity. Black women are three times more likely to code-switch, by adapting their language and communication style based on the social context or audience. LGBTQ+ women hide personal aspects five times more, and women with disabilities feel they must perform duties perfectly to avoid judgment. These experiences lead to stress, burnout and thoughts of leaving companies.

Myth #4: Only Women Want Flexibility at Work

- **Truth:** Remote work benefits all genders. Twenty-nine percent of women and 25 percent of men work remotely. Additionally, 53 percent of women and 36 percent of men appreciate the reduced pressure on personal appearance. Offering flexibility is seen as crucial for the future success of companies by half of the women and a third of men.

And Now, The Great News!

I promised you early on that while we would explore the current "state of affairs" for women in the workplace, we would primarily focus on what is within our control.

Before we get to my big reveal, let's discover **why** you want to lead.

"Ignore the glass ceiling and do your work. If you're focusing on the glass ceiling, focusing on what you don't have, focusing on the limitations, then you will be limited."
—*Ava DuVernay*

Chapter Four

Defining Your NorthStar Goal

"We must have a theme, a goal, a purpose in our lives. If you don't know where you're aiming, you don't have a goal. My goal is to live my life in such a way that when I die, someone can say, she cared."
—*Mary Kay Ash*

When you picture yourself in your ultimate leadership role, what does that look like? Are you a CEO overseeing an executive team? Are you an entrepreneur starting or taking over a family business? Are you leading a non-profit organization?

Now that you've got this picture, why does this matter to you? Is it the responsibility of carrying your organization's vision into the future? Is there fulfillment realizing that your business provides an innovative and inspiring environment for your team? Is it the knowledge that you and your team's daily actions impact countless lives in your community?

Finally, how will you feel when you get there? Does your bank account have a specific number of zeros? Will you finally have the respect you desire from parents, friends and colleagues? Will you have a sense of accomplishment or a deep understanding of your purpose?

Perhaps you haven't thought that far ahead. Maybe you've been living one day at a time. There might be a possibility that you are just thankful to have a job. That is perfectly acceptable and relatively common if you answer "yes" to any or all of the above. We have all fallen into the trap of going through the motions while the days, weeks, months and even years fly by us.

Wake up call! The days of operating on autopilot can only carry you so far. One of my favorite phrases that jerks me back to reality anytime I'm searching for the "easy" button or my fairy godmother is this:

"No one is coming to save you; no one is coming to make life right for you; no one is coming to solve your problems. If you don't do something, nothing is going to get better."—Nathaniel Branden

If you want to see your leadership dreams turn into reality, you must start with intention and the best way to do that is to help you establish your NorthStar Goal.

What is a NorthStar Goal?

Think of a NorthStar Goal as your guiding light. This goal represents your overarching purpose, vision, or aspiration. It is your ultimate destination, the big dream you want to achieve. Imagine it as the brightest star in the sky, always guiding you in the right direction. This goal is unique to you, irrespective of limits or outside influences. It helps you make choices and plans that align with your aspirations.

Just like sailors used the North Star to find their way, your NorthStar Goal enables you to stay focused on what's most important to you. Like anything worth having, it will take time and effort, but identifying your

NorthStar Goal keeps you on course, helping you reach for the stars and make your biggest dreams come true.

Defining your NorthStar Goal

There are three steps in determining your NorthStar Goal:

1. Your Anchor: Reflect on Your Core Values

Assess what truly matters to you and align your goal with your core values. This provides a sense of purpose and direction. If you have trouble nailing these down, ask yourself a few questions. You can relate these to both your work and personal life:

a. Recall your most enjoyable moments.

- What were you doing?

- Were you with others? Who?

- What made this enjoyable?

b. Think about when you felt most proud.

- Why were you proud?

- Did others share your pride? Who?

- What contributed to your pride?

c. Identify times of fulfillment.

- What needs or desires were fulfilled?

- How did these experiences give your life meaning?

- What contributed to your fulfillment?

d. Finally, determine your top values based on your joy, pride and fulfillment experiences.

- Why are each of these experiences important?

2. Your Compass: Craft Your Personal Vision Statement (PVS)

A personal vision statement serves as a concise overview of your ultimate career objective and essential qualities. It should be three to five sentences and describe how you envision the future in three to five years.

This statement is made up of the following components:

a. Your core values
b. Your key purpose or passions
c. Your key qualities or skills
d. The difference you want to make in the short and long term.

Here is an example of my PVS:

In the next 10 years, I envision dedicating myself to a professional journey guided by my core values of determination, curiosity and courage. Fueled by a deep sense of purpose, my mission is to empower and support women in achieving their goals. With a focus on cultivating the skill of confident leadership, I am committed to fostering an environment where women can thrive, break barriers and realize their full potential. Through unwavering determination, a curious mindset that seeks innovative solutions and the courage to challenge the status quo, I aspire to contribute meaningfully to the advancement of women in the workplace and beyond.

Ensure that the statement feels authentic. If you don't get that tingle when you speak it out loud, it needs to be stronger. Keep at it until it feels right!

Tip: A terrific way to keep your PVS top of mind is to have this transferred to a mousepad so it is always at your fingertips.

3. Your Map: Staying on Course

Now that we've explored core values and crafted your PVS, it is time to divide our one big goal into smaller milestones. This approach helps track progress and maintain motivation by celebrating incremental achievements. This should be broken down into weeks, months and years. Even daily actions should be established to get you one step closer to your NorthStar Goal.

This step is necessary as it:

1. Helps you prioritize and organize
2. Forces you to think through the details
3. Boosts your productivity
4. Establishes milestones, which is a reason to celebrate!

NorthStar Goal in Action

As promised, it is time to see how this concept applies, so let's bring in our friend. Sarah was an excellent individual contributor and quickly got the attention of the executive leadership team for her disciplined approach to problem-solving. Her work ethic and ability to come alongside junior team members to "show them the ropes" demonstrated that she had the qualities that fit the ideal profile for a team leader. Sarah feels a certain charge when one of these colleagues excels at a presentation or grasps a new concept. While Sarah is excited about the opportunity, she wants to ensure that this step aligns with her desire to make a significant impact on the lives of others.

Her first task is to design and implement a mentorship program for 10 junior female colleagues that the company has selected. Sarah and her organization understand that a successful program will improve retention, build connectivity, and accelerate the advancement of these women. The leadership team has empowered Sarah to use her own methods to arrive at this goal, which will run over the course of three years.

Sarah's Anchor:

Sarah has assessed what matters to her by examining her personal and professional life and has determined that her core values include empathy, development and collaboration.

Sarah's Compass:

By taking stock of these values, she is ready to craft her PVS: "Over the next three years, my personal vision is driven by core values of empathy, development and collaboration. I am dedicated to fostering an environment where junior colleagues thrive and become valuable contributors to the organization. Through empathetic leadership, I aim to understand and support their unique needs, providing guidance for their personal and professional development. By promoting collaboration, I aspire to create a cohesive team that collectively achieves success. My purpose is to empower and uplift others, cultivating a workplace where everyone's potential is realized, contributing to the growth and success of our organization."

Sarah's Map:

Sarah has established that her NorthStar Goal is to create a space for colleagues that fosters their growth and results in a group of top-performing professionals for the company.

Breaking this goal into specific milestones and daily actions allows Sarah to track progress, address challenges and celebrate incremental successes as her team gains experience and proficiency.

Goal	Short or Long Term	Estimated Completion Date
Design the Mentor Program to include the reason for the program. Outline what a successful program will look like for the participants and organization.	Short Term	Year 1
Announce the new program to the organization and begin to recruit potential mentors based on skill set and availability. Ensure each mentor understands their responsibilities and goals for the program.		
Meet with each colleague and their manager to identify any specific areas of development. Schedule one-on-one meetings with the mentees and three potential mentors to ensure the right fit.		
Kick off the program and schedule periodic check-ins with mentors and mentees to measure progress and address concerns.		
Provide quarterly Executive Summary updates to the leadership team, including wins and challenges.	Long Term	Ongoing
Celebrate achievements and recognize individual growth. Assess overall team performance and identify areas for improvement.	Long Term	End of Year 3

By reflecting on her core values and skills, Sarah's NorthStar Goal ensures that her work significantly impacts her colleagues and company and aligns with her guiding principles.

Your Turn: Establishing Your NorthStar Goal
Step 1: Identifying Your Core Values

Ready to work? Use this space to answer the following questions:

a. Recall your most enjoyable moments.

- What were you doing?

- Were you with others? Who?

- What made this enjoyable?

b. Think about when you felt most proud.

- Why were you proud?

- Did others share your pride? Who?

- What contributed to your pride?

c. Identify times of fulfillment

- What needs or desires were fulfilled?

- How did these experiences give your life meaning?

- What contributed to your fulfillment?

d. Finally, determine your top three values based on your joy, pride and fulfillment experiences.

- Why are each of these experiences important?

- Use the list of common values below or add your own:

Examples of Core Values

Accounability	Development	Independence	Perseverance
Authenticity	Empathy	Integrity	Positivity
Balance	Empowerment	Innovation	Responsibility
Compassion	Fairness	Kindness	Respect
Cooperation	Flexibility	Loyalty	Resilience
Courage	Generosity	Open-mindedness	Self-discipline
Creativity	Gratitude	Optimism	Support
Curiosity	Honesty	Patience	Teamwork
Determination	Humility		

Step 2: Crafting Your Personal Vision Statement

Use this space to identify the following:

My core values	
My key purpose or passion	
My key qualities or skills	
Where I see myself in 30 days, 90 days, 1 year, 5 years.	

Use this space to combine the above into your PVS:

Step 3: Mapping It Out

Use this space to map out your NorthStar Goal timeline:

My NorthStar Goal:

Goal	Short or Long Term	Estimated Completion

Both you and Sarah did a fantastic job with this first exercise! However, we all know things don't always go according to plan, so we will see how Sarah's strategy plays out in the following chapters.

Summing It Up

We've covered a lot of ground in Chapter Four. Let's recap how far we've already come! We have:

1. Established your NorthStar Goal

2. Identified your core values

3. Crafted your Personal Vision Statement

4. Established a timeline for achieving your NorthStar Goal

Secret: You are the NorthStar Goal for me and this book is my vessel. Do you know why I know this? Sitting here writing in the early Sunday morning hours, I cannot think of anything I would rather do! Whenever I imagine a woman breaking through a barrier and fulfilling her purpose, I get excited and motivated to press on.

In the next chapter, I will reveal the system that will not only support your NorthStar Goal but also can be used to tackle challenges in your everyday life.

Chapter Five

Introducing G-Force: From Carousel to Coaster

"I have ridden the merry-go-round and I've ridden the roller coaster. I chose the roller coaster. There is more risk, but at least you know you have lived."
—*Larry Winget*

You might not realize it now, but life is like a big amusement park and you are blessed to have an "all access" pass! The challenge is this: The ride you choose will determine how you show up and your impact on the lives you encounter each day. You can opt for the management merry-go-round, where predictability and status quo are certain, or jump on the leadership roller coaster, where excitement and exhilaration go hand in hand.

As little girls, most of us were taught that the merry-go-round was our best choice. We were encouraged to step onto the carousel and select our pony. Some of the more ambitious little girls would go for the fiercest-looking beasts. You know, the ones that had the "wild horse eye."

Other girls would opt for the brightly colored horse, and then some would take what was left, just happy to be on the ride.

Finally, there were those little girls who had no interest in a ride that merely circled around for a few minutes. Their eyes were turned to the sky and their ears tuned in to the screams overhead. They might have dragged an unwilling parent toward the platform and stood on their tippy toes to reach the minimum height requirement. These girls expected more from the ride. Our new friend Sarah is one of those girls.

As Sarah buckles in, her blood begins pumping so rapidly that she can feel it in her ears. She was excitedly looking around, studying the faces of fellow riders. Some shared the same excitement, while others had begun to turn a light shade of pea green. As the coaster begins to leave the platform, Sarah realizes that any chance to get off the ride has slipped away.

Due to gravity, the initial ascent on a coaster is slow as there is no momentum yet to propel the cars upward. She can see for miles as she reaches the summit and the view is spectacular. Just as she settles in, she realizes what goes up must come down. As the peace of the last few seconds lingers, the coaster begins to tip. It is time to leap, to grasp that last breath of air and brace for the descent.

Some riders are screaming with terror; those green friends we mentioned might have lost their funnel cake over the side, and then there is Sarah, squealing with delight, arms up and feeling the wind.

As the coaster rounds the first turn, Sarah notices that the momentum has picked up and the coaster must work harder to stay on the track. She notices her hands gripping the sides of the car to maintain balance.

Just as she starts to ease into the turn, it is time for another climb. She can see the incline and knows it will take a toll on the coaster, but guess what? This time, she moves up the hill with more speed and more momentum. Do you know why? It's gravitational force (g-force) acceleration.

Let's pause for a moment for a science lesson! I never really understood physics, but luckily, my sweet husband of 20 years does! He hated roller coasters as a child. His mother, a thrill seeker, would drag her youngest child onto the rides, and while he never admitted that tears were involved, I'm certain that a few were shed.

Years later, he visited an amusement park on a physics field trip as a high school student. Their goal was to study the g-force acceleration theory of a roller coaster. Much older and a bit less frightened, he approached the ride from a scientific place. He noted the various levels of g-force based on different points in the passage. He shared this experience with me over dinner one evening, and I immediately began to compare this theory to my journey as a leader.

Picture the initial ascent as the days, weeks, months, or even years of pushing, striving, and feeling like you are the only one grinding to rise. The gravitational pull is strong and many won't reach the top; the slope is too steep. They will stall or, much worse, backslide toward the platform.

Those who persevere to the summit have a fantastic opportunity to see the landscape from a new perspective. To view people and places they might have yet to notice while heading down and climbing. This place, while exhilarating, is not meant to be one where you reside solo, as the more people at the top with you, the more thrilling the ride.

And then there are those turns! I compare this to your first challenge as a leader, the one you didn't see coming. A statement from the team that you are micromanaging their work. A comment from a direct report that they don't feel that you are listening. This is an uncomfortable place and while it might be temporary, it can feel like an eternity while we are in it.

Before we go any further, I'll tell you a secret. I was always the girl ready for the coaster. I was never discouraged by the grind, and I had the grit to prove it. I also had the gumption to go out for new roles and take on new challenges. My struggle came in the turn, the growth place. The gut-wrenching feeling of thinking you let a team member down or that the path you were on was not the right one.

Don't worry, I still remember our friends on the carousel! So, what is happening on the ground while our fearless flyers are hurled through the atmosphere on a speeding piece of steel? Some of our little girls are still holding onto their ponies. They are sitting pretty and doing what is expected. While they might be checking the administrative and prescribed managerial boxes, no one is genuinely growing on their teams. And what about the gals that chose the wild-eyed ponies, gazing longingly up at the coaster? Maybe they are now noticing that there aren't many little boys on this ride. They realize that the real action is up there. These girls also know that deep down, they belong on the ride, that the carousel will never give them the thrill they desire.

So where are you today, my friend? Are you on the merry-go-round or the coaster? Perhaps you are on the ascent. Are you in the weeds, the trenches? Are you up with the sun and home with the dusk, where your desk begins to feel more familiar than your bed? Most women are comfortable in this place as we've become accustomed to ensuring the work is done well.

On the other hand, you could be poised on the edge of the summit. A new opportunity has been posted internally, or you've received a call from a recruiter with a plum position externally. This might be your first shot at leadership or your next logical step on the path to the C-suite. No matter where you are on the journey, the next moment will require some forward motion, an action that only you can take.

Maybe you are leaning into the turns, fumbling through the first three years as a team lead, and feeling like you need to do something else. You might even be questioning if you have what it takes to do this leadership thing long-term.

What I'm asking you to do today is to examine where you are on this ride so that we can figure out what you need to do to ensure that when you leave the park, your purpose and that of your team has been fulfilled.

This synergy that I've discovered is called the G-Force Code. Once unlocked, it becomes an unforgettable part of who you are and how you show up. It doesn't matter where you are in life—unlocking the G-Force Code changes everything, making each day more important than the last and giving you a clear purpose.

At the conclusion of each chapter in Part 2, I will provide you with one of the keys to unlock the Code and, at the end of our time together, you will have all you need to unleash your potential.

A word of caution: The roller coaster ticket comes at a much higher premium than the merry-go-round. You will be asked to give up a few things, like your free time, ego, and the fear of uncertainty. There will be sleepless nights and days when you feel like you have accidentally stumbled into the House of Mirrors.

Sound tempting? Well, here is the upside. Once you understand your true self and identify how you want to show up as a leader, your life transforms with a newfound purpose. I'm here to guide you on that journey.

I promise you, my friend, that when you discover your unique leadership abilities (and realize it isn't just about you), you will find an insane level of power and fulfillment.

So, step right up if you are ready to experience G-Force leadership, where the heart requirement replaces the height requirement, and the ride is one you will never forget.

Your Turn: How Am I Wired?
The Value of Self-Assessment

By unveiling your NorthStar Goal, we know where you want to go, but where are you today?

Self-assessment is foundational in understanding one's initial grit, growth, and gumption levels. This reflective process serves as a mirror, reflecting both strengths and areas for improvement.

Tip:

1. Answer the following questions honestly; your first response is your best response.

2. Consider your experiences, attitudes and behaviors in a professional context.

3. Use the scale provided to rate each statement.

Scoring:

- Sum your scores for the five questions in each section.

- The maximum possible score is 25, indicating an elevated level of that particular trait, while the minimum is five, suggesting room for improvement.

Grit:

How would you rate your ability to embrace and navigate unexpected changes?

1: Resistant

2: Somewhat resistant

3: Neutral

4: Adaptable

5: Highly adaptable

How well do you prioritize tasks to meet deadlines?

1: Poor

2: Fair

3: Average

4: Good

5: Excellent

How would you rate your ability to bounce back and recover when faced with setbacks or failures?

1: Less resilient

2: Somewhat resilient

3: Neutral

4: Resilient

5: Highly resilient

How would you rate your ability to collaborate within different team dynamics?

1: Inflexible

2: Somewhat inflexible

3: Neutral

4: Flexible

5: Highly flexible

How would you rate your proactivity in identifying and addressing potential challenges before they escalate?

1: Reactive

2: Somewhat reactive

3: Neutral

4: Proactive

5: Highly proactive

Total Grit Score: _____

Growth:

How do you perceive the nature of intelligence and talents?

1: Fixed

2: Somewhat fixed

3: Neutral

4: Capable of growth with limitations

5: Highly adaptable and growth-oriented

How well do you understand your strengths, weaknesses and the impact of your actions on others?

1: Limited self-awareness

2: Developing self-awareness

3: Moderate self-awareness

4: High self-awareness

5: Exceptional self-awareness

How would you rate your ability to accept and integrate feedback when receiving constructive criticism?

1: Defensive

2: Somewhat defensive

3: Accepting

4: Open to critique

5: Embraces constructive feedback

How well do you prioritize self-care to maintain your physical and mental well-being?

1: Neglects self-care

2: Occasionally prioritizes

3: Balanced approach

4: Regularly prioritizes

5: Highly prioritizes self-care

How would you rate your commitment to continuous learning and development?

1: Resistant to learning

2: Limited interest

3: Moderately committed

4: Actively seeks learning

5: Constantly pursues learning opportunities

Total Growth Score: _______

Gumption:

How comfortable are you with taking calculated risks in your professional or personal endeavors?

1: Avoids risks

2: Cautious approach

3: Balanced risk-taking

4: Comfortable with risks

5: Proactively seeks and manages risks

How confident are you in making sound and timely decisions?

1: Indecisive

2: Sometimes indecisive

3: Decisive in most situations

4: Strong decision maker

5: Exceptional Decision Maker

How often do you feel like you don't deserve your accomplishments or worry about being exposed as a fraud in your field?

1: Always

2: Often

3: Sometimes

4: Rarely

5: Never

How would you evaluate your leadership skills on a scale of 1 to 5?

1: Not confident in leadership abilities, struggle to take charge

2: Somewhat confident but hesitant in asserting leadership

3: Moderately confident, comfortable taking on leadership roles

4: Confident, actively demonstrate effective leadership

5: Extremely confident, recognized as a strong and influential leader

What percentage of the required skills and competencies are necessary when applying for an elevated job or role?

1: 50% or less, believe I only need a small percentage of the required skills

2: 51%–70%, feel I need a basic understanding but not the full range of skills

3: 71%–80%, feel I need a basic understanding but not the full range of skills

4: 81%–99%, feel I need a comprehensive set of skills to succeed

5: 99%–100%, believe I need to possess every required skill and competency

Total Gumption Score: _______

Add all three and divide the total by 75 to produce your total G-Force Score:

(Total / 75) = G-Force Score

Now rank the traits in order, with the highest trait as number one.

1.

2.

3.

Did your strongest trait catch you by surprise? Did you notice any areas that were noticeably lacking? If so, can you pinpoint instances in your career journey where any deficiency may have hindered your progress?

If so, take heart! These traits can be cultivated and honed with intentional effort and mindset adjustments. With these traits now identified, we can progress by targeting the exact area or areas requiring improvement, enabling you to overcome obstacles and achieve impactful leadership.

This book is designed much like the old Choose Your Own Adventure books we read as children. You can skip to the Growth Chapter now if your Growth Score was the lowest or if you are a rule follower, you are welcome to read the chapters as they are laid out. It's your choice!

PART TWO

Grit, Growth and Gumption for Women:

Three Keys To Lead Yourself and
Others With Confidence

Chapter Six

The Grit Factor: It's All About the Climb

"I've got a woman's ability to stick to a job and get on with it
when everyone else walks off and leaves it."
—Margaret Thatcher

G rit (noun):

1. small loose particles of stone or sand

2. courage and resolve; strength of character

As the waiter placed the plate of Gulf Coast oysters on our table, my mouth began to water. My mom and I love oysters from all parts of the country, and our favorite way to savor them is on the half-shell. That night, I did not hesitate to grab the first one off the plate and knock it back, no sauce or cracker. I felt something hard between my teeth as I chewed the little mollusk. Not wanting to make a scene, I spit the little pebble into my napkin and found that, upon inspection, it was a tiny pearl!

This was not a pearl that would end up as part of a fine piece of jewelry or on display at a museum, but a little treasure that had found its way to me. As I tucked it away in my purse, I decided to keep it as a reminder of the night. I later thought about how that tiny pearl could have started as nothing more than a grain of sand on the ocean floor. Due to the current or another force, the sand entered the oyster's center. While the oyster is doing its best to protect itself from this new irritant, it is simultaneously coating the intruder with lustrous layers that ultimately become beautiful. The sand, because of its grit, becomes the prized possession.

In this chapter, we explore the essence of grit, looking at its significant impact on women's career journeys and its crucial role in building confidence.

What Is Grit?

In career development, where various skills and strategies are praised for success, there's a force more potent than pedigree, talent, intelligence, or opportunity. That force is grit—a strong determination and relentless perseverance that pushes you through challenges and setbacks, guiding you toward your goals.

Grit is often called the "never-give-up" attitude, but it's more than just persisting. Think of grit as the stamina that helps you stay on the path to success, even when faced with difficulties, failures, or distractions. This force keeps the fire of ambition burning, guiding you through tough times and challenging situations.

What Grit Isn't

One misconception about grit is that it is how intensely, for the moment, you want something. Grit is for the long term, the long haul. It is staying in the game when you are bleeding, your lungs hurt, and you are ready to give up.

The Psychology Behind Grit

While grit has been part of the fabric of humankind since the beginning of time, it wasn't until Angela Duckworth's groundbreaking book on grit was published that it became a "thing." Her work became the focus of a TED Talk and an award-winning best-seller. One of my favorite observations from her studies is that passion and perseverance are more important than talent. I love this finding because it levels the playing field for success. Grit does not care where you grew up, what your IQ is or if you attended college. Grit only wants you to show up to the game and play your heart out for all four quarters and into OT for the win!

The intriguing aspect of grit is that it is malleable—it's not an anchored trait but rather a skill that can be developed and nurtured over time. Cultivating grit involves adaptability, self-discipline and, most importantly, resilience.

GRIT STRATEGY #1: ADAPTABILITY

Adaptability is the capacity to adjust and respond to new challenges or circumstances and is the first element of grit mastery. It involves being flexible and proactive in navigating uncertainties and evolving situations.

One thing I've come to rely on during my 25 years in business is that as a new day dawns, so do new challenges. One moment, I could have negotiated the best deal for my client, and the next hour, we received word that another client's upcoming deal was in jeopardy.

Here are three Adaptability Strategies I use when my day starts to go "off the rails":

1. Agile Thinking:

Train your mind to pivot when faced with unexpected circumstances. You can practice this by reframing situations positively and brainstorming various solutions to challenges.

To see this in action, let's check in on Sarah, who is facing a shortage of mentor volunteers for her mentorship program. Many senior leaders have responded, "I just don't have time" or "I don't have anything to offer."

Instead of accepting these responses, Sarah decides to address the challenge creatively. She reached out to the respondents who had time issues. By speaking with each leader, she learned that each of them had times of the month that were more hectic than others. She highlighted that the total hours required could be staggered or condensed during the month based on the mentor and mentee schedules.

For those with "nothing to offer," she cited specific areas where these individuals had significantly impacted the organization. She highlighted how those projects would translate into valuable teaching moments.

Sarah approached this barrier by addressing individual challenges, translating into successfully engaging mentors for all 10 colleagues. Go, Sarah!

2. Experimentation and Iteration:

Embrace the mentality of experimentation. Test new approaches, strategies or ideas, and be open to adjusting or refining them based on feedback and outcomes.

I once had the opportunity to interview with an industry publication on "The Power of Creativity." One of the main points I drove home in the article was encouraging colleagues to use their unique approaches when tackling challenging issues. Just because we have provided the same version of our company proposal to the client each year, is that the best we can offer? Can new products or services be incorporated into our presentation to enhance the client's program? Are there any new tools to make the presentation visually appealing or interactive?

G-Force Tip:

Do not wait for someone to ask you to improve the process! Take the initiative to put your own "polish and shine" on it. This can be a great differentiator and makes you stand out as someone who sees opportunities to improve around every corner.

3. Adapt to Technology:

Staying updated and proficient with technological advancements is imperative in today's competitive environment. Technology often drives change; adapting to new tools and systems enhances flexibility.

For example, we all had to learn to operate in a fully remote environment during COVID-19. Those of us who had limited videoconferencing exposure before the pandemic soon learned how to master the art of screen sharing, chat functions, and keeping our dogs from barking or children from yelling while we were unmuted. Those who leaned into teleconferencing during that time are still employing it today to meet with clients across the globe without the time or expense related to travel. We can now solve a problem with a two-hour Zoom meeting that otherwise would have entailed several days' worth of travel. Talk about efficiency!

Another example of Adaptability related to technology is using Artificial Intelligence (AI). Even those traditionally lagging industries have begun to produce tools and products that marry technology with a human touch. I use an AI tool daily to refine emails, automate repetitive tasks, and break down complex concepts into manageable information. There are countless uses and opportunities! Learn how to use this to your advantage now and you will be ahead of the curve.

Tribal Wisdom: Ride the Tide

Meet Tina Blackwell Romaine, my long-time friend and seasoned insurance professional with 25 years of experience in the industry. Her journey began in Atlanta, Georgia at a Fortune 500 insurance brokerage before returning to her hometown in the Florida Panhandle to take over her father's independent insurance agency. Over the last two decades, Tina has focused on improving and expanding the agency by significantly increasing their commercial client base, adopting new technology, and establishing relationships with new insurance carriers. Despite the challenges, including dealing with thousands of claims related to Hurricane Michael, Tina has always ensured that her clients receive the support and care they deserve. Tina credits adaptability as a key to riding the waves of change and shares three tips for adapting to a new situation or environment:

1. Cultivate an Attitude of Gratitude: It is the most essential trait to survive and thrive in any business environment. Your attitude is a choice you make consciously each day, impacting how you approach any situation. Embracing uncertainty and viewing change as an opportunity for growth can turn challenges into stepping stones.

2. Plan Ahead and Don't Be Afraid to Pivot: If you plan your business strategy in advance, you have time to change course if required. Remember that there is more than one way to solve a problem. If you find yourself stuck on a problem with no solution in sight, step away for the day and take another crack at it in the morning with a fresh mind.

3. Get Comfortable with Being Uncomfortable: Adaptability requires stepping outside of your comfort zone. Whether you are taking on additional responsibilities, learning new skills, or tackling unfamiliar challenges head-on, don't quit! You will get through the challenging times, and there will be better times ahead. Focus on your path to success and plan for it!

GRIT STRATEGY #2: SELF-DISCIPLINE

Self-discipline entails controlling actions, emotions and habits to achieve goals by staying focused, motivated and consistent despite distractions or difficulties.

Don't we all start each day with the best of intentions? We have our day designed in our minds and plan to be uber-effective. Cue the music and the chirping birds. Coffee, check. Makeup and hair, check. Commute, check. Turn on the computer, check. Open email, che.. Yikes! Six emails from the client, all before 7 a.m. "I need this asap," the subject line reads, which was the FIRST email. The last subject line reads: "ANYONE WORKING TODAY? Are you on PTO?"

At any given point, on any given day, at any given business, the client will inevitably need something from you that you had not anticipated. We must learn to expect the unexpected, account that it will take up part of our day, but then learn to turn our attention back to our planned objectives. Those colleagues I've seen who struggle with this let one email, call from the client, or comment from their manager derail THEIR ENTIRE DAY. Enter our friend Self-Discipline.

One of the best pieces of advice I received from a wise woman once was this: "Control your day, or your day will control you."

Here are a few self-discipline strategies to deploy when your day takes an unexpected turn:

1. Set Specific & Prioritized Goals:

Amidst constant changes, having a crystal-clear focus on your objectives acts as a guiding light, enabling you to direct your efforts purposefully.

Break down your goal for your week into manageable steps and create actionable plans. This approach allows you to maintain progress despite unexpected shifts, providing a roadmap to navigate changing circumstances while staying on track.

In practice, this might look like writing down the 10 most critical items you must accomplish in your week. Number the items from 1 to 10, with 1 being the most vital. Next, assign several tasks to each day of the week, ensuring that you pair high-priority and low-priority items on the same days. This balance will ensure you are not front-loading your week with all your mission-critical items.

By practicing mindful time management, you will prioritize tasks based on their importance and allocate dedicated time slots for crucial activities.

This practice will enhance focus, minimize distractions and bolster discipline in shifting priorities.

G-Force Tip:

A daily planner is crucial for effective time management, providing structure, organization, and clarity to prioritize tasks. I use the daily view of my Outlook calendar to schedule my to-dos around my meeting schedule. I use the BUSY setting to block time and prevent interruptions.

2. Cultivate Consistent Routines and Rituals:

Develop consistent routines and rituals that support your objectives. Even amidst rapid changes, maintaining certain daily or weekly habits fosters stability and discipline, creating a sense of control amid uncertainty.

I've had the honor of coaching young colleagues over the years, and one common theme I've found is that without a solid daily system in place, your day will likely run you rather than you running your day. While your manager or team lead can list assigned duties or tasks that must be accomplished daily, you have absolute control over when you perform them. I can recall a time in my early 30s when I managed a large book of accounts and felt the wave of work beginning to crash down on me. It was not a good feeling; I could not get caught up no matter how hard I tried, and each day felt like it was worsening. Looking around me, I noticed some women were in the same boat, paddling in circles. Some had resigned themselves to the feeling that this was their lot in life and had become accustomed to uncertainty. However, some women navigated the choppy waters day after day with the same amount of confidence and efficiency.

These women intrigued me. What was their "secret sauce"? It wasn't just years of experience. Some women who were masters of their desks were younger than me. It wasn't that any of the women had degrees in project management either. As I studied them daily, I realized what they had, which I had yet to possess—a system!

G-Force Tip:

If you are having trouble focusing, try using the Pomodoro Technique, which breaks work into intervals, traditionally 25 minutes long, separated by short five-minute breaks. After completing four intervals, you can take a more extended break. This technique aims to enhance focus and productivity and manage distractions by working in concentrated bursts.

Why don't we check in on Sarah to find out what her daily system looks like?

Once she is adequately caffeinated, Sarah logs into her computer and before opening ANY emails, not even peeking at them, she reviews her schedule/to-do list for the day. Next, she checks her voicemail to determine if any urgent calls had come in overnight that required returning before 9 a.m. Sarah then opens her email and tackles the most pressing client or team requests, leaving any non-urgent items for the afternoon. Sarah then uses a Pomodoro Cycle to tackle her top priority for the day, as she knows her best work is done in the morning.

Does Sarah take a break for lunch? Yes! She either takes a quick walk or grabs a bite with her coworker. The time away from her desk gives her the mental respite she needs, and she comes back to her desk with a fresh perspective. By the end of each day, Sarah has crossed off the items on her to-do list and leaves with a sense of accomplishment.

Remember, as you develop systems around self-discipline, ensure they are adaptable frameworks rather than rigid structures. Design systems that can accommodate changes and adjustments without compromising your overall objectives.

3. If You Can't Get Out of It, Get into It!

I vividly remember stepping into a new role and inheriting a desk that was mentally abandoned by my predecessor months before her departure. Her exit left behind a labyrinth of unresolved accounting issues and a backlog of tasks. I realized quickly that the only way out was to roll up my sleeves and dive in.

I dedicated myself to untangling the mess for months, day after day, nights, and weekends. There were no shortcuts or magical solutions—just sheer determination and relentless effort. Slowly but steadily, the chaos began to unravel.

With attention and commitment, I transformed the disarray into an organized and coherent book of accounts. The satisfaction of witnessing delighted clients ultimately made every sacrificed hour worthwhile.

Reflecting on that challenge, I realized no secret formula or unique shortcut existed. It was solely the investment of dedicated time and unwavering attention that paved the way to success.

GRIT STRATEGY #3: RESILIENCE

Resilience signifies the capacity to endure setbacks and recover from challenges. It involves withstanding pressures and difficulties and leveraging these experiences to bounce back, learn and grow stronger. Resilience enables you to navigate uncertainties or changes while maintaining focus.

If you have researched grit, resilience will be a concept you already know. I consider it the most essential element of grit! Without resilience, setbacks or failures might significantly impact your overall motivation, potentially leading to discouragement, decreased perseverance, or difficulty maintaining consistency in your pursuits.

Let's review a few strategies for cultivating resilience:

1. Prioritize Self-Care

Do you ever get to work and realize you are wearing two different black boots or only one earring? How many mornings have you sustained yourself on cold coffee alone? When was the last time you got eight hours of sleep? What about that annual doctor's check-in you've rescheduled three times? Whether you are a mom, a dog mom, or a caregiver for aging parents, we are often the last item to take care of on our to-do lists. Sadly, many have learned to live in this fully caffeinated, blurry-eyed state!

I am here to tell you that no one else will do it if you do not care for yourself! We can define self-care as doing things to take care of your body, emotions and mind. And guess what? Self-care is not selfish! It has been clinically proven to diminish the effects of anxiety and depression, reduce stress and increase happiness!

To have a balanced and satisfying life, it's crucial to understand self-care and make it a regular part of your routine. Whether essential daily habits or more memorable things, self-care is all about activities that help you relax, feel refreshed and grow.

Did you know that self-care is backed by science? According to a national survey conducted by Varago in 2021, respondents cited these benefits of self-care, which included increased self-confidence (64 percent), increased productivity (67 percent), and increased happiness (71 percent)[3].

What practices are included in self-care?

It can be as simple as ensuring enough sleep, eating well, exercising regularly and maintaining personal hygiene. On a broader scale, self-care includes meditation, mindfulness, journaling, pursuing hobbies and enjoying leisure activities. These activities aren't just extra treats; they're crucial for keeping a healthy balance in life.

How can I incorporate self-care into my daily routine?

Master Mindful Mornings!

A morning routine is a fantastic way to start your day. It might require setting that alarm a half hour earlier than usual, but you will crave that time once you've established a groove.

Here is a brief look at my Mindful Morning Routine:

5:45 a.m.:

- Wake up! No SNOOZE allowed! Check out some of Mel Robbin's podcasts on the 5-4-3-2-1 Rule and her hatred of that snooze button!

- Make Your Bed! This is non-negotiable. Admiral William H. McRaven wrote an entire book on how simple acts such as this can change your life.

- Brush your teeth with your non-dominant hand: Get this! You are creating new neural pathways that can enhance cognitive function by simply brushing with your left instead of your right (or vice versa) each day.

6:00 a.m.:

- Drink eight ounces of water before you get to the coffee or tea.

- Daily Devotional.

- Try some breathwork.

Tribal Wisdom: Breathe Through It!

My friend Cara Lenz is a former HR and Leadership Development expert within the tech world. Realizing her job was likely killing her; she fled corporate America and a toxic work environment to find her health. Today, she helps leaders and organizations create cultures that produce excellent results by improving the well-being of their employees. She also coaches individuals to find a balance so they don't have to decide between work and health.

Her secret? Getting down to the root cause ... your nervous system! Using strategies grounded in neuroscience, Cara helps people better understand themselves and their teams, leading to increased engagement, productivity, retention and overall happiness. The first step is your breath. Breath has shifted you from a fight-or-flight response (your sympathetic nervous system) to a relaxation response (your parasympathetic nervous system). There are several breathing techniques out there, but for Cara, the most crucial part is noticing. Most of us default to short, shallow breaths into our chest throughout the day, keeping us in that fight or flight space. And we don't even know it. Combining breathing with other strategies can be highly effective in helping you find your calm and your long-term mental health.

Here is Cara's 60-second Quick Balance Strategy to use in those challenging moments to calm your nervous system—remember BAM:

B: Breathe—Take 2–3 deep breaths into your diaphragm (your belly, not your chest) with a long exhale.

A: Affirm—Remind yourself who you want to be in this moment and what is important to you.

M: Move—Even if it's 10 jumping jacks, pushups, or a quick

30-second dance, find a way to move the energy through your body.

6:15 a.m.:

- Journaling, which consists of:

- Writing down an area I want to work on (e.g., people pleasing), stating an example, and providing an alternative to the behavior.

- Listing three things I'm grateful for.

- Identifying an area I could eliminate from my life (e.g., excessive amounts of coffee!).

- Praying for three people who need support.

- Visualization (what my ideal life looks like). This works!

- Stating my main objective for the day.

- Voicing aloud five to ten things that I know to be true about myself (e.g., I am a hard worker, I love my family).

Yes, this routine requires me to rise a bit early, but the benefits far outweigh the sacrifice.

Physical Activity

If you are anything like me, working out after a long day at the office is not the first thing on my mind when I get home. As I get older, I've realized that any movement is better than no movement. I'm seeing more studies come out touting the benefits of just 30 minutes of daily exercise. Wow! So, no need to sweat for 45 minutes on the treadmill or endure a 60-minute spin class? Find something you enjoy doing and schedule it as a non-negotiable on your calendar.

Tribal Wisdom: Disconnect to Reconnect

My friend Jessica DeAngelo is an Intuitive Business Strategist who guides leaders in overcoming obstacles and finding fulfillment in their roles and businesses. Jessica spent years working with leaders of Fortune 100 companies on sales strategies and found that sometimes the breakthrough they needed was waiting just outside their door. She has experienced first-hand the incredible benefits of spending 30 minutes in nature, while moving your body and being unplugged from technology. She now coaches her clients to do this same practice every day. Studies have shown that spending as little as 10 minutes in nature can lead to an immediate reduction in stress and anxiety. Twenty minutes can enhance your mood and wellbeing, which includes reducing mental fatigue and increasing positive effects. But 30 minutes or more is where the magic happens. When you spend at least 30 minutes or more in nature, it leads to greater cognitive benefits and a more profound sense of connection with the environment and thereby, yourself.

Jessica gives us three tips to ensure we make the most of our time outdoors:

1. Rain or shine, mud, or snow: Don't let the weather deter you. Grab your gear and get outside. The benefits far outweigh getting a little wet or muddy.

2. Disconnect from technology: Turn your phone off or on airplane mode. This is time to reconnect with yourself. If you are distracted by technology, you are not allowing the amazing benefits of this practice to take hold.

3. Commit to yourself: Dedicate this time to upholding your personal commitments. Keep in mind, they're just as significant as the promises you make to others.

Mind-Body Practices

Mindfulness and meditation are helpful ways to handle stress. These activities teach you to concentrate on the current moment, relax your mind and decrease anxiety. These techniques allow you to feel more at ease, become more aware of yourself and think more clearly.

Get Creative

Engaging in creative activities stimulates focus and resilience by providing an outlet for expression and personal growth. Men naturally do a better job of this than women. From golf to fantasy football, they realize the importance of shutting their "doer" brain off and spending time in areas they enjoy. It is up to you to allocate time for activities you enjoy. And, no, working through a bottle of chardonnay does not count! Dig out that old watercolor set and bring it to a community painting class. Join the pickleball movement. Heck, write a book while you are at it. Anything that fosters self-expression and creativity will remind you that your professional life does not define you.

Tribal Wisdom: Fuel Your Body

As a former CPA turned Health Alignment Specialist, my friend Kaitlin Borncamp understands firsthand the struggles and stress of working in a high-demand job as a finance consultant. She is best known for helping busy professionals optimize their energy so that they can look, feel and perform their best. Kaitlin marries her corporate experience with her deep knowledge of wellness. She combines it with her wisdom of sustainable habits to deliver strategies that any woman can fit into busy schedules. Here are four of Kaitlin's top nutritional hacks to keep your body in balance:

1. Balanced meals—Prioritize 20 grams or more of protein with each meal; this will ensure you are eating meals that create sustainable energy while also crowding out many foods that we all know we should be minimizing, such as processed foods that are void of protein.

2. Sleep—Sleep should be a non-negotiable for every ambitious woman (and no, you can't catch up on sleep later). Prioritize eight hours of sleep per night, even if that means missing your morning workout—sleep is that important.

3. Hydration—Busy women are notorious for not drinking enough water. Start your day with at least 10 ounces of water as soon as you wake up and aim to drink 100 ounces of water each day. Your cells depend on your hydration status—you want your cells to be hydrated like chia seeds, not dried out like raisins.

4. Morning Sunlight—Get 10–20 mins of morning sunlight in our eyeballs within two hours of the sun rising each morning. We are still uncovering how light impacts our health, but we now know that our daily energy, ability to lose weight and sound sleep dramatically improve when we get morning sunlight.

Check In with the Pro's

Staying on top of preventative care is critical to women, especially those in high-stress careers. A few of the non-negotiable visits to put on your calendar include:

- A gynecological visit

- An annual mammogram

- An eye exam

- A skin check

- At least one dental visit

By establishing regular visits, your providers set baseline health metrics and potentially head off any conditions before they become a concern.

2. Cultivate Social Support and Connection

Building a robust support system of friends, mentors and colleagues is essential to resilience. Establishing connections and seeking support from others during challenging times bolsters emotional well-being and provides a sense of community.

So much of a female's life centers around health or family-related challenges. While we could take a friendly approach to this topic, I'd prefer to tackle it head-on. I will share with you two times in my adult life when I've needed to draw from the well of support. During these times, I was required to dig into my personal grit and resilience while leaning on my family, friends and colleagues.

The first was after a miscarriage in my early 30s. Having a child was a lifelong dream of mine, so I was over the moon when I found out I was pregnant. Out of the excitement, I shared the news with close family and friends. I started thinking of names and planning the perfect nursery. Around 10 weeks into the pregnancy, I began to experience a miscarriage. The situation was devastating, and I just happened to be on a work trip when it occurred. My travel partner was terrific and made sure I was cared for at the local hospital until my family arrived. During the days and weeks that followed, I received so much support from my family, friends and boss. Returning to work was a challenge. My emotions were all over the place for the next month, but I did discover that being there was better than being alone in my house with my thoughts. I even dared to share my story with a few close coworkers and surprisingly found that they, too, had experienced a similar loss.

The second blow came 15 years later. After suffering for years with complications related to fibroid tumors and cysts, a failed ablation, and being told by my gynecologist that this was "just part of getting older," I continued to report to work each day. It wasn't until I fainted in my kitchen that I knew a visit to the emergency room was necessary. Turns out I was pretty close to dead. My blood pressure was dangerously low. Thank goodness I found a doctor wise enough to recommend a laparoscopic hysterectomy. Once again, I leaned on my network for support. As I shared the story of my menopause journey with colleagues, I quickly learned that several of my female peers were also going through this and opened up about their struggles.

The lesson I took from these health issues is that while there is extreme vulnerability in sharing such personal matters with those you work with, this can also be an opportunity to come alongside each other in support and learn more about their struggles.

Tribal Wisdom: There is Beauty in Your Journey

Stacy Huston is the Executive Director of a nonprofit that uses social networking to amplify unsung heroes and causes in communities across the United States. Stacy's personal and professional mission are aligned. She believes that we are all six degrees or less from someone or something that needs our help. Her work centers on connecting people to critical resources, sharing stories from changemakers in order to inspire the next person, and leveraging the power of celebrity to make an exponential impact.

Stacy believes there is one universal truth: In any gathering, there is not a person who will not be able to connect with at least part of the challenges we have had in our individual journeys. Whether it's grief, loss, rejection, or betrayal, there's immense power in not only embracing these challenges but talking about them. Often, our most difficult experiences are not merely obstacles to overcome but opportunities to repurpose for the greater good, offering support and understanding for others. Here are Stacy's tips on finding ways to share your challenges in a way to uplift not only your spirit but those around you:

1. Embrace Transparency with Purpose: Openly share your struggles and challenges by framing them in a context that highlights your journey toward overcoming or managing these obstacles. This approach not only humanizes you but also makes your experiences relatable, encouraging others to open up about their own struggles, thereby fostering a supportive community environment.

2. Focus on the Lessons Learned: When sharing your challenges, emphasize the lessons learned and the growth you've experienced as a result. This positive framing helps to transform the narrative from one of hardship to one of resilience and personal development. It inspires others to reflect on their own challenges in a new light and to find the valuable lessons within their own experiences.

3. Leverage Your Platform for Good: Use whatever platform you have—be it social media, community gatherings, or personal blogs—to share your stories and the stories of others who have turned their challenges into opportunities for growth and service. Highlighting these stories not only uplifts others but also amplifies the impact of your message, encouraging a culture of empathy, support, and action within your community.

3. Establish Boundaries:

Setting clear boundaries will protect your well-being, whether you call it Work-Life Balance or Work-Life Integration. Learning to say "no" is as important as saying "yes" to safeguard your mental and emotional resilience.

Here are a few ways to help:

Time Management

We all know that stress can wreak havoc on your mental state, but did you also know it can affect your physical condition? One encounter with stress landed me in my local physician's office. I had been under a great deal of stress for a prolonged period, which resulted in a horrible case of hives covering my upper body. The rash would subside overnight but reappear like clockwork as I started to work each day. When I shared this illness with my internist, she stated, "You might not need anti-anxiety medicine; you might need to look for another job." The comment was a wake-up call that prompted me to reevaluate how I was working and that I had not set healthy boundaries with my employer. I had let work creep into my nights and weekends. I was taking it home with me, mentally. I lay in bed recounting everything I had done that day and the impact it would have had if I not performed it flawlessly. The situation prompted me to get a better grasp on my time and the management of it. I realized I could still give my all during working hours, but the time I had after that belonged to myself and my family, and I should show that time as much respect. And, by the way, I did find another job!

Work-life Balance or Work-life Integration?

This leads me to the concept of work-life balance. Work-life balance involves maintaining a clear boundary between work and personal life, ensuring each gets their fair share of time. Henry Ford popularized this concept in the early 1900s, stating, "It's high time to rid ourselves of the notion that leisure for workmen is either lost time or a class privilege." Ford understood that his men were more productive when they worked shorter hours. One challenge that Mr. Ford was not up against was connectivity. The dawn of the almighty email meant we could rapidly respond to our client's needs. During the pandemic, the days seemed to blur into one long workday where most people were "on" and ready to address concerns. Enter the "work-life integration" concept, where personal and professional responsibilities are expected to be harmonious.

Work-life integration emphasizes blending work and personal life to complement each other, allowing for more flexibility and fluidity. The pandemic redefined how and where people work. Many companies offer fully remote positions, enabling staff to work from anywhere.

This is one area I have had to learn to live in as I get older. As a self-pronounced and recovering "people pleaser," my hand will shoot up to volunteer before the question is even asked. I've learned that you will do nothing well if you try to do everything. You will end up overscheduled, overworked, and exhausted.

While your goal might be to add value by taking on additional responsibilities, the result **could be several incomplete projects that are not reflective of your excellent work ethic.**

Tribal Wisdom: The Power of Positivity

Joyce Lum is a certified health and wellness coach who specializes in longevity and positive psychology. She coaches and teaches her clients that positivity goes beyond just smiling; it entails living life to the fullest. With her background as a former banking leader, Joyce is aware that women in high-pressure jobs can experience anxiety, depression and burnout, as well as physical ailments like heart problems, headaches, migraines and obesity. Women must develop mental, emotional, physical and spiritual (purpose and meaning) strategies to deal with setbacks and address such issues appropriately. Joyce shares three tips to help women cope and flourish in adversity:

1. If you make the time to take care of yourself first, by extension, you'll be taking care of others as well.

2. "You do you" because your authenticity and vulnerability will open doors to new possibilities. I promise!

3. A healthy person has a million dreams. An unhealthy person has only one. Find ways to support your mental, emotional, physical and spiritual (purpose and meaning) well-being so you can BE that healthy person.

4. Learn From Failure—There Is No Quit in Grit:

One item we need to tackle before moving further is failure. We will touch on this topic extensively throughout our journey, but I'd like to start with a personal story.

I've had a close relationship with failure my entire life. As a kid, my attempts to discover the one sport I was good at was a challenge. The sign-up fees were immense, from karate to softball, swimming to dance. I got comfortable being the last picked for ANY sport at PE and knew I would be the last to finish the fitness mile we were required to run each semester. The great news was this: failure was encouraged in my house as it meant you were trying. My mother would sit in the stands and cheer me on as I struck out or let the ball slip past me way out in right field. She'd console me on the way home: "At least you were trying and smiling!" This support allowed me to continue exploring my interests without fearing rejection from my loved ones.

What if we applied this principle to a career? A first attempt at a new task or role could present a significant challenge, followed by what you might perceive as a vast public failure. But what if we begin to socialize the idea of failure? Throughout this book, we often touch on the element of failure.

As with developing any new skill, there is the process of trying and failing. I want you to get comfortable applying failure to every aspect of your life; if you aren't failing, you aren't trying! We will refer to this concept as the FAIL FORCE, which means you are one step closer to better.

Your turn: Do me a favor and jot down a quick list of all the activities you tried as a child and answer the following for each one:

- Did you excel or struggle with this activity?

- Did you have fun or labor through the activity?

- Did you let the outcome of the activity (winning a game or successfully playing a piece of music) define who you are?

If your list is anything like mine, it would be long and riddled with many failed attempts. However, in the grand scheme, I had fun with each new experience and always kept the outcome from defining who I was. As Steven Bartlett so eloquently put it: "Failure is feedback. Feedback is Knowledge. Knowledge is Power!"

PUTTING IT ALL TOGETHER: GRIT AND SUCCESS

Now that we have explored several strategies for cultivating your grit, let's dive into what benefits you'll receive from learning to stretch and strengthen this muscle:

You'll be a more valuable contributor.

Grit transforms individuals into indispensable and invaluable assets in the workplace. Adapting, persevering, and overcoming challenges make you an essential resource to your organization and industry.

You'll be more relevant.

Gritty women stay relevant by embracing change, staying informed about developments in their industry, and actively seeking growth opportunities. This relevance enhances your professional longevity.

You'll be better equipped to face challenges.

Every industry has its challenges, requiring individuals to navigate complex scenarios regularly. Grit equips women with the mental fortitude needed to face these challenges head-on. Rather than being overwhelmed, they approach obstacles with a determined mindset, increasing their chances of success.

You'll be a better leader.

Leadership demands adaptability, self-discipline, and resilience. Women with grit naturally develop leadership qualities, inspiring and guiding their teams through challenges. Gritty leaders set an example, fostering a culture of perseverance and passion.

Your Turn: Grit in Action!

List three ways grit has helped you move you forward in the past:

1.

2.

3.

List three instances where, if you had exhibited more grit, you would have benefited:

1.

2.

3.

List three ways that you plan to apply grit:

1. This week:

2. This month:

3. This year:

In conclusion, the grit factor is a potent force for women navigating challenges. By understanding the psychology behind grit and learning how to cultivate it, women can position themselves for long-term success. The decisive choice of adaptability, self-discipline, and resilience further enhances grit and contributes to personal and professional fulfillment.

As women harness the power of grit, they not only bounce back from setbacks but also emerge as resilient leaders, better equipped to thrive in the ever-evolving landscape of their profession.

As we conclude our study of the fantastic element of grit and move into the realm of growth, I will leave you with a quote from my friend Marissa Johanson:

> *"I have learned that resilience is a major key to running a good race in this life. And this life has given me several opportunities for learning this. I find resilience blends best with equal portions of will, courage, love, curiosity, truth, and determination. Altogether, this combines to form what John Wayne referred to as true grit."*

Chapter Seven

The Growth Factor: Lean Into the Turns

> *"I learned always to take on things I'd never done before.*
> *Growth and comfort do not coexist."*
> —*Ginni Rometty*

Growth (noun)

1. the act or process, or a manner of growing; development; gradual increase

2. size or stage of development

Do you remember those early days of adolescence? Those awkward middle school years when you were changing from a little girl into a woman. If you were anything like me, it was pretty unfortunate! I'm unsure if it was the braces or the remnants of my perm, but I had a face only a mother could love. Do you remember how it hurt to deal with all the changes invisible to the outside world? During my sixth-grade year, I remember waking up at night with horrible cramps in my legs. My mom would rub my calves and comment that these were just "growing pains" everyone had to endure.

And at the end of this season of growing pains, I emerged a few inches taller and less unfortunate-looking. The funny thing is, I don't remember how intense the pain was or how many nights of sleep I lost; I only recall that I could finally fit into my older sister's clothes, much to her dismay!

That's the exciting thing about growth. While you are in a growth season, it most often feels uncomfortable. Sometimes, we choose to grow, like taking a pottery class or learning a new language. Other times, growth is not our choice, like learning to move through a difficult season in your career or working with a challenging personality.

I've already clued you into the fact that growth was the weakest trait in my early days as a leader, and I still work on it daily. In this chapter, we will define and dig into the importance of a growth mindset. We will outline strategies to learn from emotional intelligence, work on giving and receiving constructive criticism, and embrace a spirit of continuous learning and improvement. We'll also explore why continual growth is essential for career advancement and how it positions us to thrive amidst rapid changes.

What Is Growth?

Growing and expanding your skills, knowledge and abilities can shape your career as a woman. It's not just about learning new skills; it's a mindset—a promise to yourself to keep learning throughout your life and being open to change.

What Growth Isn't

A common misconception about growth is that it's always linear and consistently upward. Many believe that progress should be constant without setbacks or plateaus. Change often involves fluctuations, setbacks and periods of stagnation, which are natural parts of the journey toward personal or professional development. These moments are opportunities for learning and adaptation rather than indications of failure.

What Is the Psychology Behind Growth?

Imagine your brain is like a muscle. When you work out, your muscles get stronger. I recall when I first started doing Reformer Pilates in my early 40s. If you are not familiar with this form of exercise, picture in your mind a medieval torture device meant to stretch you and bend your body in a multitude of ways. And the crazy thing is, women pay money to work out on this thing! I felt shaky, tight and relatively unstable when I first started. After a month of consistent work, I moved through the workout at a much stronger clip. My body had become familiar with something initially unnatural. The same principle can be applied to your brain. Growth comes from a mindset, and your chosen attitude will determine the rate and depth of your development.

What Is a Fixed Mindset?

Imagine if someone thought their abilities were set in stone with no chance of improving. That's called a fixed mindset. It's like saying, "I'm not good at negotiating; I'll never be good at it." This mindset can limit what you believe you can achieve.

What Is a Growth Mindset?

Now think about the opposite—a growth mindset. This is when you believe you can improve with time, effort and practice. It's like saying, "I might not be good at negotiating yet, but if I keep trying, I'll have the client eating out of the palm of my hand." With a growth mindset, you see challenges as opportunities to learn and expand.

So, What Is Happening in Your Brain?

When you face a challenge or learn something new, your brain makes new connections with synapses like tiny bridges in your brain. New bridges (synapses) form when you learn something, like building roads in your brain to help information travel. As you keep learning and practicing, these bridges get stronger. It's similar to making those roads super-efficient so data can travel faster. Synapses also help your brain adapt to new things. When you face challenges, your brain builds new bridges to handle the information, making it more flexible and able to grow. Learning and memory are like reinforcing these bridges. The more you practice, the stronger and faster these bridges become. So, every time you learn or practice, you're not just gaining knowledge—you're building and strengthening bridges in your brain, making it more innovative and efficient!

Why Is This Important?

Having a growth mindset helps you take on challenges. Instead of giving up when things get tough, you see them as a chance to improve. This mindset makes you more resilient (remember grit) and ready to face new things.

In a nutshell, the psychology behind growth is about believing that you can improve with effort, facing challenges as opportunities, and understanding that your brain is like a muscle—it gets stronger the more you use it!

Characteristics of a Growth Mindset

Putting in the Effort:

Believing that you can develop your intelligence and abilities is a fantastic way to approach learning. Even at my age (which will NEVER be disclosed), I know this dog can learn new tricks. At the ripe age of (ha, thought you tricked me), I realize I can even write a book!

Seeking Out Challenges:

Seeing challenges rather than obstacles will help you build problem-solving skills, toughness and the ability to stay in the game longer than those who cannot adapt.

Acknowledging Errors:

Mistakes are inevitable but viewing them as learning opportunities rather than failures is a hallmark of a growth mindset. Most of us work in an industry where details matter. We are all human and will undoubtedly miss more than our share of errors. The FAILFORCE magic comes from embracing mistakes as a part of the learning process. The best leaders encourage their teams to fail forward by giving them assignments outside their comfort zone and providing a safe space for them to try. The result could be a miss or the production of an innovative solution that might save the company and the team time and money.

I had a terrific manager who consistently pushed me to try new things, assuring me he would take the blame if I failed. His one request was to always come to him first when I had made a mistake rather than try to hide or fix it alone. This is psychological safety at work, which is critical to growing your team.

Learning From Mistakes and Owning Our Choices:

This is the fun part. This is the part where I "get real" about situations and occurrences in my life where my best self did not come through, I missed the mark, or I just fell flat on my butt. This is one of those parent moments: "Do as I say, not as I do!"

My first job out of college landed me in Cleveland, Ohio. I moved to Cleveland despite having another job offer in San Francisco. Everyone, including my mom, questioned my sanity. "Why would you want to move to Cleveland, Ohio, Tinsley?!" I explained to my mother that the job offer in Cleveland was a terrific opportunity to work as a junior broker on large accounts. I had researched and found a great loft apartment in the Warehouse District, and my mind was made up. We loaded up my little Isuzu Rodeo (I miss that car) with everything it could hold and set off from Athens, Georgia, to Cleveland, Ohio.

My first few months in the Cleveland office were exciting. One thing that you should know about me is that I love being the new kid on the block. I have never met a stranger, so no matter where I go, I can make new friends and adapt quickly. I realize this is only the case for some, and something we will discuss later when we talk about getting out of your comfort zone.

As I began to settle into my new life in Cleveland, I noticed a marked difference in the culture of the Midwest versus the South. The South is like a big golden retriever, bounding up to you, asking your name, and inviting you over the next day for supper. We are instantly best friends, and I have no problem spilling all my tea about family, friends and relationships; you get the point. I found that Midwesterners prefer to take relationships a bit slower. While they may have you over for dinner, they like to keep their relationships tighter with those with whom they've formed long-standing bonds. While there is no right or wrong way, I found it challenging to find that tribe of close gal or guy pals in the new city.

While I found my work rewarding, I got very lonely, especially during the winter. If you are unfamiliar with Midwestern winters, the sky can appear grayish white from November until April. It is a bit gloomy! And not to mention the snow! So here I am, alone in my apartment, desperately homesick and longing for community. After a year and a half and much internal debate, I decided it was time for me to come back home to Georgia. Fortunately, my office leader found a way for me to transfer within the company to an open position in our Atlanta office. The only thing left was telling my manager that I was going. To this day, the disappointment on his face is still burned into my mind. He asked me to give it a few months to settle in and acclimate to the environment. He wanted me to consider the possible opportunities I might give up by leaving. I let him speak his mind, but there was no changing mine. I was back in Georgia by the spring and loving my new life in Atlanta.

What is my point in telling you this? It is twofold. First and in hindsight, I could have given that town more time. I could have trusted my manager's word that, in time, I would settle in. Did I miss opportunities that could have sent my career in a different direction? Possibly. While there is no changing the past, which, by the way, I wouldn't if I could, the lesson here is that if you are willing to make a massive shift like moving to a new town for a job, make sure you give yourself enough time to settle in and understand that while you might be seeking refuge in the familiar people and places you always knew, there are so many benefits to giving a new home a fair shot. Second, we all will make choices we must live with, and some might not work out as expected. The secret is to own those choices, knowing you did the best you could at the time with the information you had.

A growth mindset can benefit individuals and the teams they serve. By creating a safe place where questions are encouraged and mistakes are acknowledged, you, as a leader, will find that your teams have creative and innovative solutions to problems where other teams struggle. The team will find greater satisfaction and fulfillment in their work with the awareness that they are driving the change. For more information on this topic, check out Carol Dweck's groundbreaking TED Talk to learn about the growth mindset.

GROWTH STRATEGY #1: EMOTIONAL INTELLIGENCE

Emotional Intelligence is recognizing, understanding, managing and effectively using your emotions and those of others. This was my biggest shortcoming regarding my early days in leadership, which is common. This is an area where many leaders need to catch up, yet it still needs to be a cornerstone of traditional leadership training. Mastering this area can be a secret weapon, but failing to address a lack in this area can be your Achilles' heel.

According to the World Economic Forum's Future of Jobs 2023 report[4], "the socio-emotional attitudes which businesses consider to be growing in importance most quickly are curiosity and lifelong learning;

resilience, flexibility, and agility; and motivation and self-awareness—evidence that businesses emphasize the importance of resilient and reflective workers embracing a culture of lifelong learning as the lifecycle of their skills decreases."

Recent studies have also found that people with high emotional intelligence (EI) make an average of $29,000 per year more than people with low EI.

It is likely that these trends will continue for years to come, so it will benefit all of us to get this right!

Here are a few strategies to help increase how we relate to others:

Self-Awareness and Self-Regulation (Know Yourself and Control Yourself):

Recognizing and understanding your emotions includes being able to name your feelings accurately. We have all known, and maybe have been, that person who sends a snarky email, complains about a team member, or, even worse, flies off the handle in a moment of frustration.

Managing your emotions, staying calm, and not reacting impulsively are not only expectations of your role as a leader at work but also of the expectations of your leadership style outside of work.

I have seen instances of lousy behavior unchecked in organizations because the individual was a high-ranking executive or a "key" employee. Let me say with all confidence that by letting this behavior go unchecked, you are not only sending a message to that person that what they are doing is acceptable based on their ranking or work product but also to your team that their security and well-being come second to the work.

If you encounter this on your team, the best approach is to address it with the person immediately and provide an action plan to help them prevent future issues.

Tribal Wisdom: Learn Yourself to Lead Yourself

My friend Melani Luedtke-Taylor is a pretty impressive human! She is a TEDx Speaker, best-selling author, and MBA with over 25 years at leading Fortune 500 companies. Melani knew early on in her journey that while the title of "manager" held little value, the title of "leader" came with great responsibility. Melani now has the privilege of focusing on building the next generation of leaders, and emotional intelligence is her specialty. Here are Melani's four tips to strengthen your EI muscle:

1. Negative self-talk is a defeater of progress. When you catch yourself thinking, "I am not good enough" or any other negative statement, stop yourself. Instead, think, "Would I say those words to someone else?" The answer will likely be "no," so why are you saying them to yourself? Turn it around into a positive statement.

2. Ask yourself WHY instead of allowing frustration to seep in. If your emotions are getting the better of you, ask yourself, "Why am I experiencing these emotions? What triggered this response?" If someone else is a challenge, ask yourself, "Why is he/she behaving this way?" Understand why this allows for logical thinking and empathy rather than an impulsive, emotional response.

3. Have an emotional outlet and practice it daily. Journaling, jamming to music, dancing, painting, snuggling with a pet or whatever you enjoy that allows you to release any pent-up energy.

4. Be kind to yourself, always. Feeling guilt temporarily can bring about positive change. However, excessive guilt is linked to anxiety and depression. Feel enough to make a positive move forward and then move forward. Do not dwell on mistakes made.

Team Skills (There Is No I in Team)

The adage "there is no I in team, but there is a me" still rings true today. The most valuable part of a team is the strength of each of its players. Each person brings their unique skill set and experiences to the table, and it is our job as leaders to ensure everyone understands their critical role.

With the advancement of technology, organizations now engage with clients, suppliers and colleagues worldwide. This entails navigating various workplace work ethics, languages, traditions and cultures to foster collaboration without causing friction or tension among team members.

Tribal Wisdom: Leading Without Borders

Michelle Roberts is renowned for her intercultural expertise with over a decade of diverse industry experience, including women's leadership. She specializes in guiding through international leadership challenges. Here are Michelle's three tips when leading a team of people from diverse backgrounds:

1. Be Curious. You're in a whole new world—an unfamiliar environment, whether you've moved to a different town, state, or country or lost your job, promotion, or loved one. Look around. Take in the things you've overlooked. Observe. Channel your inner child and ask, "Why?" Walk (physically or metaphorically) through your new environment and ask questions. The more you learn about the people and places around you, the more you learn about yourself.

2. Be Creative. Life as you know it is now different. Or your life isn't different, and you realize it's not what you want. How are you going to find your way? Get back on track? Don't edit your thinking. Let your imagination run wild. Talk to people who are doing things that you find interesting. This is where creative thinking uncovers the many possibilities and opportunities at your fingertips. If you're unable to stay on the career track you were on, what do you want to do?

Something completely different? Go back to school? Change professions? Become a tennis star? Or do you want to find a way to continue on your path, but that exact path is no longer available? Find ways to do something related or adjacent to the position you were in. Use this time to hone skills to help you reach the next step.

3. Be Courageous. It's time to step out and step in. Step out of your comfort-ish zone, the place you're hanging out right now. I say "comfort-ish" because you're probably not really enjoying it, but it's what you know. And being in a mental/physical place we know is comforting. It's time to get comfortable with being uncomfortable. And step in; step into who you are and were meant to be.

4. And along the way, don't forget to celebrate!

Conflict Resolution:

No matter how much care you put into developing a team that works cohesively, inevitably, conflicts will arise, and it will be your responsibility as a leader to assist in a solution.

Conflict resolution entails understanding the root cause of the issue, empathizing with all parties involved and collaboratively finding a solution that satisfies everyone's needs and interests. This involves effective communication, active listening, negotiation and sometimes mediation.

As Sarah prepares for a team-building event as part of her Mentor Program, she learns that two of her team members are at odds. This stems from the fact that a mentor tapped one team member to accompany them on a critical client visit while the other was asked to stay at the office. This created tension between the two team members based on resentment. Sarah chose to find out more from the mentor based on the choice and learned that the team member selected for the visit had reached out previously to express interest in more client-facing opportunities. Sarah then scheduled a meeting with the two team members to discuss the issue, explain the reasoning, and follow up with all the mentees with a survey to gauge their interest in exploring more client-facing roles. Sarah's approach showed the team that she was swift in resolving the conflict and cared about their individual goals.

The ultimate goal is to reach a resolution that preserves relationships, promotes mutual understanding and fosters a positive environment for collaboration and growth.

Learning to handle conflict demonstrates the ability to lead effectively and create a positive workplace where everyone feels valued.

Empathy (Understand Others):

In my early days as a manager, I struggled with empathy. I loved my team hard; they knew I would protect them at all costs. My problem was that I thought they needed me to fix their problems or share a similar struggle that I had experienced with them and tell them how I dealt with it. In hindsight, I realized that what they needed from me was less mouth and more ears. This is still a struggle for me as a reformed "fixer," but I have tried to develop my level of empathy by listening more and talking less. I give my team members the space to share and discuss the issue. Sometimes, they will solve a problem by just talking through it, but occasionally, a solution is unavailable. The magic lies in you just being there. Not to fix, not to recommend.

Learning the decision-making style of each person on your team is also beneficial. For example, I have a strategist, two teachers, and an analyst on my team. I encourage them to lean into these natural abilities regularly and have learned how to pair them up within our team or with external groups, which results in fantastic collaboration. Each of these women possess unique communication styles, and I've learned how to frame my communication with them to ensure optimal results.

An elevated level of emotional intelligence can empower you as a leader by enhancing your interpersonal skills, communication abilities, and overall effectiveness in leading and managing teams. Plus, you create a positive work culture, equating to a happier and more innovative group.

G-Force Tip:

Create opportunities for team members to engage in volunteer activities together outside of work. Whether it's participating in a community service project, organizing a fundraiser, or volunteering at a local charity, these experiences can foster empathy by allowing colleagues to connect on a deeper level while making a positive impact in the community. Working together towards a common goal outside of the office can strengthen bonds, build trust, and enhance empathy by providing new perspectives and shared experiences beyond the typical work environment.

GROWTH STRATEGY #2: THE POWER OF CONSTRUCTIVE CRITICISM

Have you ever been on the receiving end of someone's "constructive criticism" and walked away feeling like the scum of the earth? It could be that the person was just there to criticize, and nothing was "constructive" about it. Genuine constructive criticism focuses on the positives and the negatives to provide beneficial and clear actions for the recipient to improve. This practice can provide different viewpoints and reveal blind spots we cannot see. As a leader, you are responsible for effectively giving and receiving constructive criticism graciously.

Here are a few tips to help navigate the process:

How To Ask for and Receive Constructive Criticism

Soliciting feedback regularly shows a commitment to growth and improvement. You can request this from colleagues, mentors or other leaders to gain valuable insights. Be prepared to get what you ask for and receive it with an open mind. By not taking this personally or becoming defensive, you can ask clarifying questions and seek specific examples. This will demonstrate to the giver that you value their opinion and plan to take actionable steps to improve.

How To Give Constructive Criticism

The key to providing constructive criticism is to do so in a supportive, specific, and actionable manner. The person should never feel under attack. The OIILS method of providing feedback is an acronym that stands for:

1. Observation: Begin by stating specific observations or actions you observed. This makes the feedback concrete and actionable.

2. Impact: Describe the impact or consequences of the observed behavior. This helps the recipient understand the effects their actions have on others or the situation.

3. Inclusion: Include the recipient by inviting their perspective or input. This fosters open communication and encourages collaboration in finding solutions.

4. Leverage: Suggest ways to leverage strengths or improve weaknesses based on the observed behavior. This helps the recipient understand how they can build on their strengths or address areas for improvement.

5. Sustain: Lastly, discuss how the behavior can be sustained or improved over time. This ensures that the feedback leads to long-term growth and development.

The OIILS method provides a structured approach to giving feedback that focuses on specific behaviors, their impact, collaboration, improvement and sustainability.

Let's break this method down using Sarah.

Observation: Sarah recently noticed that her colleague, who was once stellar, has started missing essential details in her assignments.

Impact: This oversight has affected the quality and reliability of the work, potentially causing delays or errors.

Inclusion: Sarah could approach her colleague to discuss if there are any challenges or changes that may have led to this shift in performance.

Leverage: They could explore strategies together to address the issue, such as implementing checklists or scheduling regular progress check-ins.

Sustain: It's important for Sarah to provide ongoing support and feedback to help her colleague maintain high-quality performance in the long term.

Constructive Criticism in Practice

One of the best practices we employ on my team is honest communication. I am fortunate to have surrounded myself with a group of women who are far brighter and more insightful than I hope to be. One of the best aspects of my team is the immediate feedback they provide. When I make a less-than-stellar decision about the direction of a project or make a comment rooted more in opinion than logic, it takes little time for it to come to the surface. The great news is that I am less likely to do the same thing twice. It also makes me aware that my team and those around me observe my actions as I move through my day, so I better act with sound and fair judgment.

G-Force Tip:
Do you know the old saying, "Opinions are like..."? It will save you tons of time and anguish to learn to discern between constructive criticism aimed at your improvement and rude, unproductive comments.

In summary, mastering the art of receiving, delivering, seeking, and effectively utilizing constructive criticism allows you to tap into its power for evolution, refining abilities, and attaining tremendous success for yourself and your team.

GROWTH STRATEGY #3:
A LIFETIME OF LEARNING AND DEVELOPMENT

Your brain is one of your most significant assets! While our hands spend hours on the keyboard daily, this beautiful and complex organ directs our thoughts, so why not maximize it? Weighing in at only three pounds, the brain contains one hundred billion neurons. According to a survey from 2013, around 65 percent of Americans believe that we only use 10 percent of our brains. Barry Gordon later explained this myth in Scientific American that while most of the brain is almost always active, the brilliance comes in how much POTENTIAL your brain has.

Why Is This Important?

It is your responsibility to develop your skills to match the needs of your current position and also stretch your abilities toward those required to achieve your NorthStar Goal.

If you are trying to reach your NorthStar Goal, consider learning to be the fuel to carry you closer. By embracing the idea of continuously acquiring new skills and knowledge, you add value and create an edge others will not have. The more you learn, the more confident you will become in your work.

There are many learning avenues, so commit to investing in yourself. Here are a few ways to do that:

Learning at Work

Take advantage of learning opportunities at your current company. Many companies offer training programs and workshops to help employees acquire new skills. Express your interest in professional development to your supervisor or the HR department and inquire about any available training initiatives. Many companies sponsor or give bonuses to acquire advanced degrees or designations. Additionally, consider participating in on-the-job projects that allow you to learn and apply new skills in a practical setting.

Learning Online

Dive into the world of online learning! Numerous platforms offer courses, from technical skills like coding to soft skills like leadership and communication. Websites like Coursera, LinkedIn Learning, and Khan Academy provide accessible and flexible opportunities for women to enhance their professional skills at their own pace.

Tribal Wisdom: Your Competitive Advantage

My friend Natalia Motoc is widely recognized as an expert in the staffing industry, possessing a background in recruiting, client relations and operations. She knows exactly what it takes to stand out from the crowd. Two of her biggest pillars are willpower and habits in all you do. Willpower gives you the opportunity to perform at your best and habits make you the most disciplined person on earth (even though many say it's vice versa).

Here are Natalia's tips to ensure you stay ahead of the pack:

1. Maintain and Develop Your Skills: Regularly assess the skills needed for your current role and future aspirations. Communicate with your employer to understand the expectations of your role. Attend workshops, pursue certifications, and stay informed about emerging trends. By consistently upgrading your skills, you position yourself as a valuable asset to your organization, setting the stage for career acceleration.

2. Add Value to the Company: Creating value goes beyond meeting job requirements. Identify ways to contribute meaningfully to your organization's goals and objectives. Take on additional responsibilities, propose innovative solutions, and actively seek opportunities to make a positive impact. When your contributions align with the company's success, you become an indispensable part of the team, enhancing your chances for advancement.

3. Improve Interpersonal Skills: In any industry, interpersonal skills are paramount. Strengthen your communication ability, build relationships and navigate challenging conversations by being emotionally sober. Developing strong interpersonal skills enhances your professional reputation and positions you as a leader who can effectively collaborate and inspire others.

4. Exceed Expectations: Consistently exceeding expectations is a surefire way to stand out in a competitive environment. Go above and beyond in your role, take on challenging projects and deliver exceptional results. By consistently surpassing expectations, you demonstrate your commitment to excellence and position yourself as a top performer worthy of advancement.

5. Recognize Your Worth: We often underestimate our worth and unintentionally conceal our true value out of fear of others' reactions, opting to remain in the shadows. It's time to break free from this self-imposed limitation and boldly assert your worth.

GROWTH STRATEGY #4: THE POWER OF MENTORS, SPONSORS AND NETWORKING

My manager is always putting my name in the hat for that promotion, right? Not always and that's not their sole responsibility. I once had the delusion that my manager took note of every win my team experienced or every solution I was delivering for the organization. Surely, they saw the results and regularly discussed my amazing leadership skills, right?

The truth is, while your manager does take note of your accomplishments, skills and potential, you need to be proactive in ensuring that you are connecting with other professionals, both in and outside your industry, to help with your growth and to showcase your talent.

Let's explore a few of the relationships that are critical to develop in your leadership journey:

Mentors

Mentors offer guidance based on their experiences, helping you navigate your career path and acquire new skills through their wisdom. Selecting a mentor is crucial for women as it provides invaluable support in navigating unique challenges you will encounter in the workplace. Mentors offer guidance on overcoming gender bias, building confidence and developing essential skills. They play a pivotal role in empowering women, serving as role models and providing insights into career advancement.

What Should I Look for in a Mentor?

Experience

A seasoned mentor can share their journey, highlighting the pitfalls to avoid and the shortcuts to success. By tapping into their wealth of experience, mentees can navigate challenges more effectively and make informed decisions that contribute to their career advancement.

Emotional Support

Whether dealing with a problematic client, overcoming a team setback or balancing work and personal life, a mentor offers a supportive ear and valuable advice. The emotional connection forged through mentorship creates a sense of belonging and resilience, empowering women to face challenges head-on.

Career Development Planning and Accountability

A mentor can assist you in crafting your NorthStar Goal as part of your development. Regular check-ins create a sense of responsibility and motivation. Knowing that someone is invested in your success can drive you to strive for excellence and meet objectives. This accountability factor boosts individual performance and contributes to a positive, goal-oriented organizational culture.

Mentorship fosters a proactive approach to career development, ensuring women are well-prepared for the challenges and opportunities. A mentor is a crucial ally, offering guidance, encouragement and practical insights to propel women forward in their professional journeys. Moreover, mentors open doors to networking opportunities and introduce women to valuable connections within their industry.

Your turn: Jot down three people who you would consider approaching as a possible mentor, why they would be a good candidate and when you plan to reach out to them.

Sponsors

How is a sponsor different from a mentor? A mentor provides guidance, feedback and support, while a sponsor actively promotes you to decision-makers, endorses your skills and recommends you for opportunities. A sponsor holds power and influence, understands your work and invests in your career. To find a sponsor, identify suitable candidates, typically senior-level executives. Then, build a relationship, showcase your value and request their sponsorship.

What Can a Sponsor Do for My Career?

Think of a person as the one who sings your praises when you are not in the room and ensures you are on the radars of critical decision-makers. Ensure that your sponsor clearly understands your NorthStar Goal, along with any areas you are working on developing. Ensure you deliver only the highest quality work and show gratitude for this instrumental individual.

Your turn: Is there someone within your organization that is currently sponsoring you? If not, jot down three people who you would consider approaching as a possible sponsor, why they would be a good candidate and when you plan to reach out to them.

Networking

Networking provides valuable insights into various fields and opens doors to collaborative learning. Here are a few benefits:

Access to Resources and Opportunities

Building a robust professional network opens doors to many resources and opportunities. Relationships matter in every industry and a strong network can provide access to key decision-makers, industry events and exclusive opportunities. Through strategic networking, women can position themselves as valuable organizational contributors, gaining visibility and recognition.

Knowledge and Expertise Sharing

Networking facilitates the exchange of knowledge and expertise. Engaging with professionals from diverse backgrounds exposes women to different perspectives and innovative approaches. Attend industry conferences, join professional associations and actively participate in networking events to broaden your horizons. By sharing insights and staying informed about industry trends, women can enhance their expertise and contribute meaningfully to their organizations.

Increased Confidence

Effective networking builds confidence. As you expand your network, you will develop vital interpersonal skills and the ability to communicate confidently. Meeting industry leaders, participating in discussions, and presenting ideas in various forums contribute to a sense of empowerment.

Your turn: What type of networking events align with your NorthStar Goal? Are they industry-specific or related to a certain set of skills? Seek out at least one networking event per month and schedule it as a non-negotiable event on your calendar.

Tribal Wisdom: Form a Personal Board of Directors

My friend, Alexis Cierra Vaughn, is an accomplished insurance expert, serving as the Founder & Chief Executive Officer of a firm committed to strategy consulting and bespoke e-learning training platforms for insurance agencies and Insurtechs. Alongside her leadership in the company, Alexis excels as a sought-after keynote speaker, an educator in insurance technology, and a podcast host, all while nurturing her growing family.

Central to Alexis' journey is her reliance on a select group she calls her "Personal Board of Directors." This trusted circle comprises individuals who have significantly influenced her growth and continue to provide invaluable guidance. Acting as a diverse network of advisors, they offer varied perspectives and constructive feedback essential for decision-making and personal advancement. Through ongoing engagement, these individuals assist Alexis in overcoming challenges, staying focused on her objectives, and advancing toward her aspirations.

Alexis offers three tips when selecting your Personal BOD:

1. Select a person who has achieved a position at the level you aspire to reach in your career journey.

2. Identify a mentor who has previously occupied your current level and is capable of guiding you through the challenges and uncertainties you face.

3. Choose an advisor who can offer personal guidance, such as strategies for achieving genuine work-life balance or harmony.

Your Turn: Growth in Action!

Now that we have explored several strategies for fostering your growth, let's dive into an exercise to get your wheels turning!

Reflecting on Growth

List three ways growth has helped you move you forward in the past:
1.
2.
3.
List three instances where, if you had invested in growth, it would have been beneficial:
1.

2.

3.

List three ways that you plan to apply growth:

1. This week:

2. This month:

3. This year:

In summary, the strength of growth comes from having a flexible mindset that welcomes challenges, focuses on knowing oneself, appreciates always learning, and understands the value of strong mentors and networks. By encouraging this way of thinking, women can handle any challenge with confidence and dedication to always getting better. In doing this, they move forward in their careers and help bring new ideas; the journey to professional growth isn't a straight line but an exciting process that happens through having the right mindset, developing skills, and establishing relationships.

Chapter Eight

The Gumption Factor: The Summit and Beyond

"You might never fail on the scale I did, but some failure in life is inevitable. It is impossible to live without failing at something unless you live so cautiously that you might as well not have lived at all—in which case, you fail by default."
—*JK Rowling*

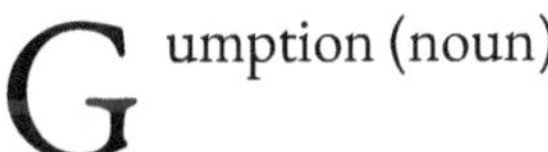

Gumption (noun)

1. initiative; aggressiveness; resourcefulness

2. courage; spunk; guts

Gumption is not a word that is used regularly in today's vernacular. The first time I recall hearing it used was in my favorite romcom, "The Holiday," when Iris, our hero, stated, "I think what I've got is something slightly resembling gumption!"

What is Gumption?

Gumption is about having the courage to take calculated risks, adjusting your approach when things don't go as planned, and staying genuine and open even in tough situations. It's about being bold, strategic and authentic all at once.

The Difference Between Guts and Gumption

Gumption and guts are two words that are often used interchangeably, but they actually have distinct differences. "Guts" usually refers to the willingness to take bold action in the face of fear or danger, often associated with bravery or courage in risky situations. On the other hand, "gumption" encompasses bravery and includes elements of resilience, resourcefulness and determination in facing challenges. Gumption involves a strategic approach to taking calculated risks and navigating obstacles with purpose and authenticity. In contrast, guts may imply more of a spontaneous or automatic response to a situation.

I've taken several risks in my life, and a few have been less than strategic. In my early 20s, I took a brief break from the insurance industry to assist a family member in running a small construction material supply company. This was when I questioned my future in the industry and realized I could have used the assistance of a strong mentor and a solid NorthStar Goal!

Without a proper diligent effort, I jumped into selling our construction product to contractors throughout the Southeast. The first year of the business boomed, and I amassed what I considered a small fortune. Little did I know that would end when what we would now refer to as a "supply chain issue" halted production of our product. The raw material used to make our product was in high demand in other countries, so our "mom and pop" operation was sunk. I learned two lessons almost overnight: (1) There is immense value in planning, and (2) Family business is not for everyone!

I needed a job and had six dollars in my checking account! Six. Whole. Dollars. Not only was my poor decision-making affecting me, but also the fate of my poor husband. I could have freaked out. I could have called my mother for money. I had to figure something out, quickly! I contacted an old professor for guidance (power of your network), who helped me identify an opportunity with a national insurance carrier in Florida. Within a month, I moved, started a new career chapter and began rebuilding my brand in the insurance industry.

This story highlights the difference between taking an intelligent risk versus a highly uncalculated one! In this chapter, we will explore strategic thinking as a critical factor in career growth. We will discover what it means to take a calculated or "smart" risk, handle decision-making challenges, deal with failures, call out our biggest enemy as female leaders and explore an untapped leadership superpower. First, let's delve into some data about women and risk-taking.

A 2019 KPMG Women's Leadership Study: Risk, Resilience, Reward[5] explores the perspectives of more than 2,000 females. The study emphasizes the importance of women taking risks and being self-assertive to advance in leadership roles. The study reveals that while 69 percent of women are open to small career risks, only 43 percent are willing to take more significant risks for career advancement. Interestingly, women's readiness to take risks decreases with experience, with 45 percent of those with less than five years' experience open to significant risks compared to 37 percent with 15+ years. Women of color are more inclined toward risk-taking (57 percent) than white women (38 percent). Women are far more likely to attribute success to good work habits—such as working hard, being detail-oriented and being organized (hello, grit!). And they are less likely to cite other, more personal, character attributes—such as being strong-willed or a good leader.

How do we change this narrative? I've outlined five strategies to help you step out confidently the next time opportunity knocks on your door.

GUMPTION STRATEGY #1: CALCULATED RISK AND REWARD

Risk-taking is a fundamental element of personal and professional development. In any industry, unforeseen challenges often arise, and embracing risks becomes a prerequisite for growth.

As I mentioned earlier, not all risks are created equal. A calculated risk means thinking carefully about what might happen and deciding to proceed after looking at the facts. This section looks into figuring out and sorting risks, telling the difference between intelligent risks and risky moves without thinking. We will also explore the psychological and professional benefits of stepping outside your comfort zone, exploring new opportunities, and embracing challenges.

Balancing Risk and Reward

While risk-taking is essential, balancing risk with potential rewards is equally crucial. It is important to weigh the potential benefits against the uncertainties, ensuring that calculated risks align with broader career objectives. To do this, we need to learn the decision-making steps in the process:

1. Start with Your NorthStar Goal:

Viewing any endeavor within the context of your NorthStar Goal will guide your decision-making process and provide a framework for assessing the potential risks and rewards. Ask yourself, does this get me closer to my NorthStar Goal? If the answer is "no" or even "maybe," you may need to reevaluate your reason for entertaining it in the first place.

2. Evaluate Opportunities:

If you've answered "yes" to the above, the next step is to research and analyze the risk thoroughly. This could include market data, industry trends and your strengths and weaknesses. This initial assessment will help you understand a particular decision's potential benefits and risks.

3. Assess Risks and Benefits:

Evaluate the potential risks involved in a decision and weigh them against the expected benefits. This is the old "risk v. reward" model. Consider both the immediate and long-term consequences of making an informed decision. As you gather information and options, consider placing these in a spreadsheet. This will help organize the data and make it easy to present to others for feedback.

4. Seek Advice from Your Mentor, Sponsor and Network:

Consulting with this group will provide valuable insights. Their experiences and perspectives can offer a well-rounded view of the potential risks and help you make more informed decisions. This support system can offer guidance, encouragement and resources that will help bolster your confidence and provide assistance in overcoming challenges.

5. Develop Contingency Plans:

Plan for potential setbacks by creating contingency plans—a Plan B. Having alternative strategies in place can help mitigate risks and provide a safety net if things don't go as initially expected.

6. Start Small:

Begin with more minor, manageable risks before tackling more significant challenges. This allows you to gain experience, build confidence, and refine your risk-taking abilities. Remember, practice only makes perfect if the procedure is done correctly!

G-Force Tip:
Acknowledge and celebrate your successes! Recognizing and appreciating your achievements boosts confidence and encourages a positive attitude toward future risk-taking endeavors.

Tribal Wisdom: The Power of Positivity

My friend Marissa Johanson is no stranger to decision-making. In her career as a Critical Care, Emergency, and Flight

Nurse, one wrong decision can make the difference between life and death for those in her care. While caring for her patients, she has had to collaborate with multiple disciplines and has discovered strategies to achieve desired outcomes. She coaches leaders to embrace the risk of being misunderstood, understanding that leaders must exercise patience and allow others the necessary time to learn from and about them. This process, combined with courage and mentorship, leads to achieving excellent outcomes.

Marissa provides three tips to help you make better decisions:

1. A Healthy Brain: Healthy self-care is complete with good quality, restful sleep, wise, healthy nutritional choices and outdoor exercise. All these yield the best option for a clear, healthy brain, which one MUST have to lead oneself and others.

2. Good Quality Questions: This is key to getting good information and one cannot make a good decision based on poor quality information.

3. High-Fidelity Listening: Spend more than just the time required to hear the words said. Listen to replies to truly understand them. Good leaders are aware of this because they have heard with this intention. Rightly understood, the group being led is more willing to apply their best efforts toward accomplishing the work.

GUMPTION STRATEGY #2: PIVOTING FROM UNSUCCESSFUL RISKS

Say you've followed all the steps to take a calculated risk, and it doesn't work out. It stinks, I know from experience! What are the next steps you need to take to keep moving forward (FAILFORCE):

1. Stay Positive

As we stressed in our chapter on grit, resilience in the face of setbacks is a hallmark of successful individuals. Maintaining a positive mindset when confronted with the fallout of unsuccessful risks can pave the way for a quick recovery.

2. Evaluate Your Approach

Objectively assess the strategies and decisions that led to the unsuccessful outcome. Break each step down to see where a different approach could have made a difference. There is value in introspection to evaluate a different system for the future.

3. Learn From Your Mistakes

As I mentioned earlier, mistakes are inevitable, but their actual impact lies in the lessons they impart. Turning failures into stepping stones opens the possibility for future growth.

4. Be Bold and Pivot!

So it didn't work out this time. Don't sweat it! Be open to pivoting when circumstances demand. Everything truly does work out in your favor.

I recall a time in my career when I applied for a big promotion. I poured months of preparation into my presentation for the interview and spent countless hours working on my development to ensure I was equipped. At the end of the process, I learned that while my interview and skill set were quite impressive, the job would go to someone else. While this was a hard blow to my ego, in hindsight, I am thankful that it worked out the way it did. This provided a great opportunity to dig into the work I was already doing and open myself up to different opportunities.

Another thing I did was accept the decision tactfully, which made a big difference in the eyes of those making the choice. How you respond to a setback is just as important as how you react to a triumph!

Your turn: Take a moment to reflect on a risk that you took in your career that did not work out exactly like you thought it would. How did you handle it? What did you learn about yourself?

GUMPTION STRATEGY #3:
BE YOUR AUTHENTIC SELF

Of all the challenges female leaders face today, one is the most significant barrier to our growth. This has nothing to do with societal limitations and everything to do with our minds. The enemy of female progress can be summed up as impostor syndrome.

Imposter syndrome is a psychological phenomenon where individuals persistently doubt their abilities despite evidence of their accomplishments and competence and fear being exposed as fraud or undeserving of their success. It can affect anyone, regardless of their gender, but research suggests that women, including female leaders, are disproportionately impacted by impostor syndrome.

What Does Imposter Syndrome Look like and What Are the Proposed Solutions?

Problem: What People Think: Societal expectations and stereotypes about gender roles can create added pressure on women in leadership positions. Women may feel they need to meet higher standards or prove themselves more than their male counterparts, leading to self-doubt.

Solution: Know that you are enough! As I told you, you are a unique creature here for a reason. As a wise woman once said, "Haters gonna hate!"

Problem: Not Enough Women: In fields traditionally dominated by men, women in leadership roles may feel isolated or like they need to belong. This sense of being an outsider can intensify feelings of inadequacy.

Solution: This is where the value of your network comes in. While you might be the only woman in a particular situation within your company, chances are other women in your industry or network may face the same challenges. Reach out and build that tribe of support.

Problem: Trying to be Perfect: Women face societal expectations to be perfect or near perfect in various aspects of their lives. This pressure to excel in all areas can contribute to impostor syndrome, as female leaders may fear falling short of unrealistic standards.

Solution: Perfect is boring and a complete façade! Own each messy step you take along your journey and encourage each woman in your network to do the same.

Problem: Thinking Success Is Luck: In cases of success, women may attribute their accomplishments to external factors like luck, help from others, or easy tasks, downplaying their competence. Conversely, they may internalize failures, attributing them solely to their shortcomings.

Solution: I love the Bruce Springsteen quote, "When it comes to luck, I make my own." Bruce was trying to convey that success is no accident. Can you imagine how many guitar practices it took for The Boss to perfect "Born in the USA"? Remember to not underestimate the power of consistent effort and own the work that you have put in.

Problem: Comparing Yourself: Comparison can hinder personal and professional growth.

Solution: Comparison, like perfection, will do nothing for your leadership skills except leave you inept. Focusing on your strengths and goals rather than comparing yourself to others is critically important. Also, compare yourself to who you were yesterday and ask yourself, "Am I working to improve today's version?"

Problem: Ignoring Compliments: Women may downplay positive feedback or dismiss praise, believing they don't deserve it. Conversely, they may internalize criticism more intensely, reinforcing their impostor feelings.

Solution: Own your accomplishments! Next time someone congratulates you on an excellent presentation, rather than responding with "It was nothing" or "It wasn't good enough," how about trying "Thank you! It took a ton of effort, and I'm proud of the work."

Tribal Wisdom: Be Unapologetically You

Jenn Gomez excels in guiding high achievers to map out and reach their objectives precisely and quickly. She has two decades of event management and logistics expertise and is passionate about steering leaders toward clear, actionable goals. Jenn champions authentic leadership, urging professionals to embrace and express their true selves. Below are her top three strategies for leaders to fully realize their potential:

1. Stop trying to be what you THINK people want you to be: The first step to overcoming imposter syndrome is to stop molding yourself into what you think others expect. Embrace your unique skills, experiences and values. Authenticity resonates more than perfection. You build genuine connections and establish trust more effectively when you are true to yourself.

2. Cultivate self-awareness: Invest time in understanding your strengths, weaknesses and triggers. Self-awareness is the foundation of gumption; it allows you to navigate challenges with confidence and grace. Reflect regularly on your achievements and areas for growth. This practice helps to ground your sense of self and reduces the power of imposter feelings.

3. Seek constructive feedback, not validation: Shift your focus from seeking constant approval to seeking constructive feedback that fosters growth and learning. Surround yourself with mentors and peers who challenge and support you. This environment encourages resilience and helps you to internalize your accomplishments, reinforcing your authentic self.

Let's check in on Sarah, who is currently having a rough time. She has been invited to represent her company at a leadership conference and will be included on a panel of six women who are touted as the industry's rising stars.

While honored to be included in the forum, Sarah begins to doubt her ability to contribute. Most of these women have MBAs or other leadership credentials. Some have already risen to the C-Suite level or are standard fixtures in industry publications for their expertise.

Sarah is so worried about the conference that she almost declines the invitation. Lucky for Sarah, she recognizes that the little voice she hears in her head is that of self-doubt. She decides to sit down and list all her outstanding accomplishments over her short time in the industry, including the programs she launched and the young lives she has impacted. She also takes another step to reach out to the other panelists to establish a relationship. She is delighted to learn that even a few have experienced pre-conference jitters. When the conference rolls around, Sarah shows up poised and ready to share her knowledge with others. So proud of you, Sarah!

GUMPTION STRATEGY #4: VULNERABILITY: THE SUPERHERO TRAIT OF FEMALE LEADERS

In today's environment, companies seek leaders who inspire and guide their teams toward a shared vision. Female leaders who demonstrate strong leadership skills, strategic thinking, and the ability to articulate and execute a compelling vision are highly valued. There is one trait, however, that is not celebrated often but takes an immeasurable amount of courage. That, my friends, is vulnerability.

While Brené Brown made vulnerability a household word as part of her viral TED Talk, it is not a concept that is widely celebrated in all organizations, even though it should be.

Understand that vulnerability is not a sign of weakness or an opportunity to divulge every mistake you've ever made.

Here are two ways you can lean into this powerful trait:

1. Building Trust and Credibility

Vulnerability builds trust. Being authentic and transparent about challenges and aspirations fosters trust amongst teams. Trust is the foundation of strong professional relationships, and credibility follows closely. Women who demonstrate vulnerability while maintaining a commitment to excellence gain the respect and trust of their peers, positioning themselves as reliable and capable leaders.

2. Learning From Experience

Acknowledging vulnerability is also a strategic way to avoid future mistakes. By seeking feedback and learning from experiences, women can proactively address areas of improvement. This approach prevents recurring errors and demonstrates a commitment to professional development.

Tribal Wisdom: Vulnerability

My friend Jean Atman specializes in empowering female leaders to liberate themselves from the constraints of past trauma, imposter syndrome, self-sabotage, and toxic relationships. Armed with a Bachelor of Science degree in Psychology, Jean guides those trapped by past pain and societal expectations that do not resonate with their true selves. Central to this transformative journey is recognizing and harnessing the power of vulnerability. Here are Jean's three tools to embrace this superpower:

1. Recognizing vulnerability as a strength. Acknowledge that vulnerability fosters genuine connections and deeper relationships. When you allow yourself to be vulnerable, you invite others to do the same, creating authentic connections based on mutual understanding and empathy.

2. Radical self-acceptance allows freedom. Many people go through life feeling "less than" based on limiting belief systems and past conditioning. When you can find yourself as a unique individual meant to lead through your specific gifts, you step into your greatness and set an example for others to do the same.

3. Embrace curiosity as your closest ally. By approaching all aspects of yourself with curiosity instead of judgment, you unlock the freedom to express your true self. Curiosity ignites a journey towards deeper self-awareness, empathy for others and a broader understanding of the world, enhancing your abilities as a leader.

By owning your missteps and providing a safe space for your team to do the same, you create an environment that allows for open communication, enhanced creativity and innovation. Have you ever shared something with a team member that made you feel completely vulnerable, only to discover they had also experienced it? If so, what happened next? I'll bet that a connection was formed almost immediately that had not existed prior. That is some vulnerability-magic if I've ever seen it!

Your Turn: Gumption in Action!

Now that we have explored several strategies for building that gumption muscle, let's dive into an exercise to get your wheels turning!

Reflecting on Gumption

List three ways gumption has helped get you to where you are today:

1.
2.
3.

List three instances where, if you had shown more gumption, it would have been beneficial:

1.
2.
3.

List three ways that you plan to apply gumption:

1. This week:
2. This month:
3. This year:

As we conclude this exploration of gumption, we recognize that women may sometimes exhibit less confidence in embracing risks that entail the possibility of failure. However, we must acknowledge that such risks are essential for leadership and achievement. It is through experiencing failure, embracing our authenticity, and vulnerability that we unlock incredible power. By fully living in our identities and advocating for ourselves, we establish a groundwork for progress in our careers and in guiding others.

PART THREE

Grit, Growth and Gumption for Women:

Three Keys To Lead Yourself and
Others With Confidence

Chapter Nine

Bringing It All Together to Unleash Your G-Force

Wow! While we have only been together a short time, it has been an intense ride! If you are anything like me, the "windblown" hair look after the coaster ride is less than attractive.

However, you look MARV-A-LOUS. What I am envisioning right now is a you that has arrived back at the platform standing up a bit straighter and maybe a bit out of breath.

Every lock has a code, and we've explored three powerful keys to unlock your most confident leadership-self. Before sending you off on your next adventure, I want to give you some bonus points to show how grit, growth and gumption intersect with each other and naturally flow as part of G-Force:

G-FORCE INTERSECTION #1: PROGRESSION

When we combine grit and growth, we are moving toward a state of progression, which signifies that we are advancing and moving forward. The magic lies in the continuous development process, learning, and ascending the stages toward your NorthStar Goal. Enhancing your skills, attaining new accomplishments, and moving to higher career levels are integral aspects of progression. Each step taken symbolizes a positive transformation or milestone, emphasizing the continuous journey of improvement and achievement along your professional path.

G-FORCE INTERSECTION #2: EXPANSION

The combination of growth and gumption results in expansion, characterized by the exploration of new opportunities. Expanding your career involves stretching your skills and experiences beyond familiar boundaries. Embracing new responsibilities, acquiring diverse knowledge and venturing into unfamiliar territories provide avenues for growth. Like a balloon expanding with air, your career broadens as you tackle challenges, experiment with innovative approaches and push yourself to evolve in various dimensions. The journey of expansion in your career revolves around widening your horizons and enhancing versatility in your professional life.

G-FORCE INTERSECTION #3: RESOLVE

The merger of grit and gumption gives rise to resolve, which is emphasized by finding solutions and overcoming challenges. Confronting difficulties in your job requires determination and courage, characteristics inherent in resolve. Intensity, persistence and problem-solving become critical components in navigating obstacles. When facing a challenging situation at work, having resolve entails not succumbing to adversity but rather figuring out solutions to propel forward. Resolve as part of your career journey mirrors adopting a can-do attitude and a steadfast commitment to addressing challenges directly.

Now that you understand the keys, strategies, and intersections of G-Force, have you determined what areas to focus on first to achieve your NorthStar Goal? It may be one singular key similar to my growth challenge, or perhaps you need to dial up your grit or gumption levels to reach a new milestone. You should know that having grit, growth or gumption on their own will not allow you to be a successful or effective leader. It is the intersection of all three that is the magic of the G-Force Code.

As we conclude this chapter and reflect on the journey we've embarked on together, it's clear that the principles of grit, growth, and gumption intersect to form a powerful force for unleashing your true potential.

Now armed with a deeper understanding of how these concepts intersect and complement each other, you have the tools to chart the course toward your NorthStar Goal with confidence and determination. Whether focusing on refining your grit, embracing growth opportunities, or summoning the gumption to tackle challenges head-on, remember that each step you take is a testament to your resilience and commitment to personal and professional growth.

Chapter Ten

The Grace Factor: A Parting Gift

Wait! Don't go yet! Don't forget your parting gift.. You thought it was a toaster oven, right? There is only one catch to this gift, my friend: You are going to give this gift to yourself!

This gift is spelled G-R-A-C-E.

Giving yourself grace means embracing perfection as a myth, especially when you are an emerging leader. As we've touched on many times throughout our journey together, society throws expectations at us like confetti and trying to fit into those molds only takes you further away from your NorthStar Goal. It's about time we acknowledged that making mistakes is part of the gig. Instead of beating ourselves up, let's cut ourselves some slack, learn from the hiccups, and keep moving.

The magic sauce in grace is this: When you give yourself a break, you're not just doing it for yourself. You're setting the vibe for your whole team. Know this: Your team doesn't need a superhero; they need a relatable leader. Showing them that it's okay to be human, to stumble and rise, creates a workplace where everyone can bring their A-game without the pressure to be flawless. So, here's to embracing the messy, imperfect and downright real you—because that's what made you a kickass leader in the first place!

With Love and Light,

—Tinsley

P.S. You didn't think I'd say goodbye without checking in one last time on Sarah, did you? I'm happy to report that the Mentorship Program was a tremendous success in her region and Sarah was asked to oversee the program's installation countrywide. Her ability to lead authentically and confidently resulted in her promotion to Senior Vice President and she continues to impact the lives of future female leaders today. Go, Sarah!

Words to Live By

The G-Force Tribe wants to leave you with a few final words of wisdom. Here are a dozen powerful ways to remove barriers and confidently lead. Review these daily until they become part of who you are and what you do.

1. Keep Your NorthStar Goal in Sight— Jenn G.

"I knew I wanted to be in the Baton Rouge 40 Under 40 in 2023. I made sure everyone I knew was aware of my intention, especially those mentors and sponsors in my network. By openly sharing my goal, I not only held myself accountable but also harnessed the power of a supportive community. Their guidance, feedback, and endorsements were instrumental in turning my vision into reality. This journey taught me the invaluable lesson that clear goals, combined with a strong network, pave the way for remarkable achievements."

2. Hold Yourself Accountable—Jessica D.

"If you're going to commit to something, the results you will get will directly correlate to your commitment level. So, for example, if you commit to the HIKE 31 challenge and decide to bail if it's raining or just not convenient that day, you won't reap the true benefits of the challenge, which is all about true connection with yourself. Find a method of accountability for yourself. It could be a good friend, posting on social media, or sharing your goals with your partner or spouse. Once other people know about your goals, you'll find you feel a deep responsibility to stick to them."

3. Practice Self Care—Cara L.

"If burnout is killing you, literally or figuratively, take note. Take charge of your health. Without it, you have nothing. Become devoted to yourself and your well-being before it's too late. Take accountability for how you feel, even if your employer doesn't. Learn. Invest in your mental and physical health. Try new things. Find out what works best for your beautiful, individual body and mind. And then devote yourself to Leading Yourself Well to be the best for those you care most about."

4. Give to Grow—Stacy H.

"The way to grow your power is to give it away. Your heart is at the center of your power."

5. Be Your Authentic Self—Kaitlin B.

"One day, I was on a call with three male colleagues I had never met before. We all went around to introduce ourselves, each of them was of a higher rank and from Ivy League schools. I immediately heard my inner critic start to doubt what value I would be able to add to the call, questioning 'who was I' as a less experienced manager with the education from a state college on a call for a topic I was sure they knew more than me. Fortunately, my urge to speak up overcame my inner critic and ended up providing many answers and most insightful information on the call. It was a valuable lesson I learned to never underestimate myself before I even start. I doubt those men remember what college I went to (or didn't go to) or even what I said, but they'll remember the impression I left."

6. Check Your Emotional Intelligence—Melani T.

"I rarely insert my opinion first during team brainstorming sessions as people have a tendency to agree with the most senior-level person in the group. I prefer to let my team drive the train and witness how the diversity of thought in the group can naturally arrive at a solution."

7. Realize the Power of a Mentor—Joyce L.

"Seek out a mentor early on in your career. Having different perspectives on strategies will help you navigate the challenges you are facing rather than figuring it out the long and hard way. Don't be afraid to seek a mentor who can guide your growth and development."

8. Learn to Use Technology to Your Advantage—Natalia M.

"Embracing technology and mastering the power of AI opens the door to endless possibilities, driving efficiency, innovation, and inclusive progress in every facet of our lives."

9. Trust Your Intuition—Jean A.

"Your intuition speaks to you through your emotions and gut feelings. It will never lead you astray. The challenge comes in getting out of your head and getting into your body where clarity is obvious."

10. Embrace the Power of Diverse Teams— Ukeme J.

"We are at a point in our country where we need unifiers. We need visionaries. And sometimes the least amongst us are the people that do that. This is because they experience a slice of the community that you're not aware of, that you don't know that you could never know."

11. Success is not Linear—Alexis V.

"The twists and turns of your career make sense if you are moving forward. Everyone's journey to success is different, with some people getting there faster and others taking longer routes. It's important to remember that setbacks and challenges are expected, and by staying determined and flexible, we can still achieve our goals."

12. Life Is like a Roller Coaster—Tina R.

"Life can't always be perfect. Don't dwell on the low points; focus on your path to success in the future. Plan your success, stick with it, and you will get there."

Set your intention to practice these principles daily until they become second nature in your personal and professional life; your future is unlimited.

So, stand a bit taller, embrace your newfound swagger, and let the harmony of G-Force guide you as you continue your journey toward achieving your dreams.

Acknowledgements

It takes a village to raise a child, and in the same vein, it takes a village to write a book! Behind Grit, Growth and Gumption lies a community of family, friends, mentors and peers, each offering encouragement, feedback, and inspiration throughout the writing journey.

- To my wonderful family. You have been here every step of the way. Steve, Ella, and JoJo: Thank you for making dinner, giving me the time and space to write, and, most of all, for your amazing support. Scout: Thank you for being my emotional support poodle!

- To my friends. Thank you for checking in on me, sending me notes and texts of encouragement and letting me test out my theories on you!

- To the fantastic men and women of the business community who poured your love, wisdom, and hard truths into me over the last 25 years. Your mentorship has been invaluable on my journey.

- To the faculty and staff at the University of Georgia's Terry College of Business. You laid a foundation for my career and remained steadfast in your promise to aid in my career. To Dr. Rob Hoyt, your guidance over the years has remained the top career advice I've received.

- To my Purpose Family. You helped me gain the courage and clarity to start this journey.

- To my Defining Moments Family. You helped this book come to life! Thank you for all your guidance!

- To Miss Tillie: Thank you for showing every woman the greatness that lies within her.

- To coffee: You are my spirit animal. We did this together.

- To my Lord and Savior. You are the reason that this book exists! I had no idea what to do when You planted this seed in my heart. Your spirit guided my thoughts, and your steadfast love strengthened me. My understanding of my role on this earth is limited, but my faith in Your Plan for my life is unshakable.

Meet the Author

Tinsley English

Tinsley is a renowned operations leader, keynote speaker and creator of the G-Force Code, a system that empowers women to embrace their true leadership abilities. With over a decade of experience mentoring high-achieving women, Tinsley uses a straightforward approach to quickly overcome challenges and nurture genuine leadership rooted in resilience and determination.

Tinsley has extensive experience in the global insurance sector, spanning two decades. She holds a Risk Management and Insurance degree from The University of Georgia's Terry College of Business and Certification in Driving Transformation Through Innovation and Resilience from Emory University.

Tinsley is a frequently featured media personality recognized as an authority on female leadership and previously served on the board of a non-profit organization dedicated to women's empowerment.

In her spare time, Tinsley enjoys the outdoors, spending time with family and making new friends.

Let's Stay Connected!

Head over to https://linktr.ee/tinsleyenglish for links to my website, social media handles and to learn more about the G-Force Tribe!

Share Your Story:

We all have our own stories of grit, growth and gumption! I would love to share your story on my website. Please email me at tinsley@gforcecode.com. Selected stories will be shared on my website.

Notes

CHAPTER 1: WHAT NO ONE IS TELLING YOU

[1] More than half of adults (51.57%) haven't read a full book in over a year https://wordsrated.com/american-reading-habits-study/

CHAPTER 2: LEADERSHIP MYTHS DEBUNKED

[2] Women in the Workplace: 2023, Report (Lean In and McKinsey & Company, October 2023) https://www.mckinsey.com/featured-insights /diversity-and-inclusion/women-in-the-workplace

CHAPTER 6: THE GRIT FACTOR: IT'S ALL ABOUT THE CLIMB

[3]Self-care is backed by science—Varago Study: 2021

https://www.vagaro.com/news/press-release/survey-finds-three-quarters-of-americans-believe-self-care-activities-provide-stress-relief

CHAPTER 7: THE GROWTH FACTOR: LEAN INTO THE TURNS

[4]The socio-emotional attitudes—World Economic Forum Study: 2023 WEF_Future_of_Jobs_2023.pdf (weforum.org)

CHAPTER 8: THE GUMPTION FACTOR: THE SUMMIT AND BEYOND

[5]KPMG Women's Leadership Study: 2019 https://info.kpmg.us/news-perspectives/people-culture/kpmg-womens-leadership-study.html

About

DEFINING MOMENTS PRESS

Built for aspiring authors who are looking to share transformative ideas with others throughout the world, Defining Moments Press offers life coaches, healers, business professionals, and other non-fiction or self-help authors a comprehensive solution to getting their books published without breaking the bank or taking years. Defining Moments Press prides itself on bringing readers and authors together to find tools and solutions.

As an alternative to self-publishing or signing with a major publishing house, we offer full profits to our authors, low-priced author copies, and simple contract terms.

Most authors get stuck trying to navigate the technical end of publishing. The comprehensive publishing services offered by Defining Moments Press mean that your book will be designed by an experienced graphic artist, available in printed, hard copy format, and coded for all eBook readers, including the Kindle, iPad, Nook, and more.

We handle all the technical aspects of your book creation so you can spend more time focusing on your business that makes a difference for other people.

Defining Moments Press founder, publisher, and #1 bestselling author Melanie Warner has over 20 years of experience as a writer, publisher, master life coach, and accomplished entrepreneur.

You can learn more about Warner's innovative approach to self-publishing or take advantage of free training and education at: MyDefiningMoments.com.

Defining Moments

BOOK PUBLISHING

If you're like many authors, you have wanted to write a book for a long time, maybe you have even started a book ... but somehow, as hard as you have tried to make your book a priority, other things keep getting in the way.

Some authors have fears about their ability to write or whether anyone will value what they write or buy their book. For others, the challenge is making the time to write their book or having accountability to finish it.

It's not just finding the time and confidence to write that is an obstacle. Most authors get overwhelmed with the logistics of finding an editor, finding a support team, hiring an experienced designer, and figuring out all the technicalities of writing, publishing, marketing, and launching a book. Others have written a book and might have even published it but did not find a way to make it profitable.

For more information on how to participate in our next
Defining Moments Author Training program, visit
www.MyDefiningMoments.com
Or
email support@MyDefiningMoments.com

Other #1 Bestselling Books

BY DEFINING MOMENTS ™ PRESS

Defining Moments: Coping With the Loss of a Child
—Melanie Warner

Defining Moments SOS: Stories of Survival
—Melanie Warner and Amber Torres

Write your Bestselling Book in 8 Weeks or Less and Make a Profit —Even if No One Has Ever Heard of You
—Melanie Warner

Become Brilliant: Roadmap From Fear to Courage
—Shiran Cohen

Unspoken: Body Language and Human Behavior For Business
—Shiran Cohen

Rise, Fight, Love, Repeat: Ignite Your Morning Fire
—Jeff Wickersham

Life Mapping: Decoding the Blueprint of Your Soul
—Karen Loenser

Ravens and Rainbows: A Mother-Daughter Story of Grit, Courage and Love After Death
—L. Grey and Vanessa Lynn

Pivot You! 6 Powerful Steps to Thriving During Uncertain Times
—Suzanne R. Sibilla

A Workforce Inspired: Tools to Manage Negativity and Support a Toxic-Free Workplace
—Dolores Neira

Journey of 1000 Miles: A Musher and His Huskies' Journey on the Century-Old Klondike Trails
—Hank DeBruin and Tanya McCready

7 Unstoppable Starting Powers: Powerful Strategies for Unparalleled Results From Your First Year as a New Leader
—Olusegun Eleboda

Bouncing Back From Divorce With Vitality & Purpose: A Strategy For Dads
—Nigel J Smart, PHD

Focus on Jesus and Not the Storm: God's Non-negotiables to Christians in America
—Keith Kelley

Stepping Out, Moving Forward: Songs and Devotions
—Jacqueline O'Neil Kelley

Time Out for Time In: How Reconnecting With Yourself Can Help You Bond With Your Child in a Busy Word
—Jerry Le

The Sacred Art of Off Mat Yoga: Whisper of Wisdom Forever
—Shakti Barnhill

The Beauty of Change: The Fun Way for Women to Turn Pain Into Power & Purpose
—Jean Amor Ramoran

From No Time to Free Time: 6 Steps to Work/Life Balance for Business Owners
—Christoph Nauer

Self-Healing for Sexual Abuse Survivors: Tired of Just Surviving, Time to Thrive
—Nickie V. Smith

Prepared Bible Study Lessons: Weekly Plans for Church Leaders
—John W. Warner

Frog on a Lily Pad
—Michael Lehre

How to Effectively Supercharge Your Career as a CEO
—Giorgio Pasqualin

Rising From Unsustainable: Replacing Automobiles and Rockets
—J.P. Sweeney

Food—Life's Gift for Healing: Simple, Delicious & Life Saving Whole Food Plant Based Solutions
—Angel and Terry Grier

Harmonize All of You With All: The Leap Ahead in Self-Development
—Artie Vipperla

Powerless to Powerful: How to Stop Living in Fear and Start Living Your Life
—Kat Spencer

Living with Dirty Glasses: How to Clean those Dirty Glasses and Gain a Clearer Perspective Of Your Life
—Leah Montani

The Road Back to You: Finding Your Way After Losing a Child to Suicide
—Trish Simonson

Gavin Gone: Turning Pain into Purpose to Create a Legacy
—Rita Gladding

The Health Nexus: TMJ, Sleep Apnea, and Facial Development, Causations and Treatment
—Robert Perkins DDS

Samantha Jean's Rainbow Dream: A Young Foster Girl's Adventure into the Colorful World of Fruits & Vegetables
—AJ Autieri-Luciano

Live Your Truth: An Arab Man's Journey In Finding the Courage to Live His Truth As He Identifies as Gay and Coping with Mental Illness Paperback
—David Rabadi

Unstoppable: A Parent's Survival Guide for Special Education Services with an IEP or 504 Plan
—Raja B. Marhaba

Please, Excuse My Brave: Overcoming Fear and Living Out Your Purpose
—Anisa Wesley

Drawing with Purpose: A Sketch Journal
—Rick Alonzo

NY Coffee: Love Fulfilled in the Little Things
—Craig Lieckfelt

Good Work: How Gen X and Millennials are the Dream Team for Doing Good When Collaborating
—Erin Kate Whitcomb

Rescue Me: Guided Self-Healing for First Responders: Conquering Depression, Anxiety, PTSD & Moral Injury
—David Hogan

Treasures In Grief: Discover 7 Spiritual Gifts Hidden in Your Pain
—Lo Anne Mayer

We Three: Their Beginnings
—Derek Drummond

Ripping off the Mask
—Joseph Lee
Culture Spin
—Kristy Wachter
Discover Your Inner Leader
—Mamta Goyal